CRITICAL INCIDENT STRESS
AND
TRAUMA IN THE
WORKPLACE

RECOGNITION... RESPONSE... RECOVERY

GERALD W. LEWIS, Ph.D.

ACCELERATED DEVELOPMENT INC.
Publishers
Muncie   Indiana

CRITICAL INCIDENT STRESS AND TRAUMA IN THE WORKPLACE

Technical Development: Cynthia Long
Marguerite Mader
Sheila Sheward

DISCLAIMER

While the information in this manual is based on clinical data, research, and experience, it is general in nature and represents only the views of the author.

Library of Congress Cataloging-in-Publication Data

Lewis, Gerald W., 1950-
    Critical incident stress and trauma in the workplace :
  recognition, response, recovery / Gerald W. Lewis.
       p.   cm.
    Includes bibliographical references and index.
    ISBN 1-55959-054-8
    1. Job stress. 2. Psychic trauma. 3. Psychiatric emergencies.
  4. Industrial psychiatry. I. Title.
    RC963.48.L48   1994
    155.9'3--dc20   93-48262
                                     CIP

LCN:93-48262
ISBN: 1-55959-054-8

Order additional copies from

ACCELERATED DEVELOPMENT INC.,
PUBLISHERS
3808 West Kilgore Avenue, Muncie, Indiana
47304-4896
Toll Free Order Number 1-800-222-1166

*In loving memory of
my dad,
Myron "Mike" Lewis*

PREFACE

In 1990, after spending several years speaking, teaching, and responding to critical incidents, I endeavored to write a manual on the subject of Critical Incident Stress and Trauma.

My objective was not to do another dissertation with zillions of quotes from mega-zillions of references documented with pages of footnotes. Also, another objective was not to use obscure multi-syllabic words but rather to provide relevant information.

The feedback from those who purchased copies of the manual was very positive and forthcoming and I was extremely grateful. I took that feedback, as well as feedback from a second (October 1991) and third (June 1992) version plus new debriefing experiences, and included those insights in this book. In addition, I have included material that was generated from the training workshops and consultation that I have conducted during the past several years.

The material presented is the result of the research of others in combination with my own impressions from my work in this relatively new field. Whenever possible, I attempted to cite the source of a quote or material in the body of the manual. Readers may then refer to the bibliography if they choose to gather more data from the original source.

Although the book may be of interest and assistance to individuals in private practice, the content was not written for those whose primary professional focus is a clinical practice. My goal was to write a *nuts and bolts* manual that would be of assistance to professionals who (1) are employed as Emergency Service Professionals (police, fire, hospital, crisis worker); (2) deal directly with victims of trauma in the workplace; (3) provide assistance to Emergency Service Professionals; (4) work in school systems; (5) work in acute psychiatric settings; (6) are Employee Assistance Professionals; and (7) may work in some manner with persons who are experiencing acute trauma and crisis.

Gerald W. Lewis, Ph.D.

September 1993

TABLE OF CONTENTS

LIST OF FIGURES

Chapter 1

UNDERSTANDING STRESS AND STRESS MANAGEMENT

The word "stress" has been around for a long time, but it has certainly become a buzzword since the 1980s. In *Webster's International Dictionary*, we find a definition of **stress**: "A physical, chemical or emotional factor that causes bodily or mental tension and may be a factor in disease causation." Simply translated: Stress may hurt us, contributing to our becoming physically as well as mentally ill.

GENERAL CONCEPTS OF STRESS

The research that has resulted in stress becoming such a buzzword is very extensive as well as conclusive and may be summarized in seven concepts:

1. Stress is a by-product of any change.

2. Since there are different types of changes that we experience, there are different types of stress; loosely defined as good stress (**eustress**) and bad stress (**distress**).

3. Not all stress is harmful. We need stress in our lives in order to feel fulfilled, excited, challenged, and ultimately satisfied.

4. Different individuals have varying degrees of tolerance for different types of stress and may perceive the same event(s) with differing amounts of stress.

5. Long-term distress is damaging to one's emotional and physical well-being.

6. Different professions have more stress than others and therefore may be considered more hazardous.

7. We have much control over the impact of stress in our daily lives; however, we generally choose not to exercise this control.

BIOLOGICAL RELATIONSHIPS

Let's take a brief sojourn into introductory biology. This may seem rather basic to many of you, but please bear with me.

The human body, and all its functions are controlled by two parts of the Central Nervous System (CNS). One part, the parasympathetic nervous system, controls the voluntary, conscious aspects of bodily functioning: moving limbs, speaking words, reading, singing, dancing, etc. The other component, the sympathetic nervous system, controls all of the nonvoluntary, unconscious bodily functions such as heart rate, respiration, blood vessel dilation, hormonal secretion, digestion, etc. This latter system is considered very primitive, dating back to a time when we were still running through the jungles and swinging through the trees. It is the part of the brain that we have in common with the monkeys, apes, dogs, etc. It is an internal mechanism that keeps our bodies functioning at the correct RPMs for whatever task we need to perform. It is the system that promotes the *fight or flight response.*

For thousands of years, this part of our central nervous system was extremely important and well-utilized as humans found themselves in situations that required that they either fight or flee. This part of the CNS would *kick in* automatically with very little conscious thought. Since it operates primarily on sensory stimulation, which is connected to the most primitive part of the brain, all it would take is the sight of an enemy or the smell of a large dangerous animal, and the individual's body instinctively would downshift into overdrive. Likewise, this system also has a braking mechanism in order to slow down the process.

As the human species has become more *civilized* and domesticated, we are no longer in many situations that allow the expression of the ***fight of flight response***. However, because it is nonvoluntary, unconscious, and connected to the primitive part of the brain, the sympathetic nervous system is still functional. We now find ourselves in situations where we have to suppress the response because to allow its expression might result in severe repercussions. Nevertheless, the internal unconscious adjustments and changes continue to go on even though the external action is suppressed. One might say that it is the equivalent to putting your car in drive and depressing the gas pedal while keeping on the emergency brake. All of the previously mentioned functions continue: heart rate, respiration, digestion, hormonal secretion, perspiration, neurotransmitter production, etc.

Let's look at what happens to an animal that is feeling threatened, about to get into a fight, or needs to flee from an enemy. The following takes place concurrently in a matter of a moment in the form of a reflexive unconscious response. Anyone who has a cat or dog will be familiar with the following scenario.

1. Adrenalin gets pumped into the blood system along with a higher level of blood glucose. This acts as a *supercharge* or *turbo boost* to the entire physiological system.

2. The stomach secretes more digestive juices in order to process any remaining food and transform it into needed energy/fuel. As part of this process, the animals excretory functions increase in order to be rid of *excess baggage* that may slow it down.

3. The heart and lungs start to increase their functioning. Breathing becomes shallow as well as rapid while the heart pumps blood at a more rapid rate.

4. Peripheral blood vessels constrict and blood is directed away from the extremities (hands, arms, legs, feet) and into the

internal organs. Once again, in the case of a fight, this is an appropriate response because it limits the bleeding that may be caused by cuts or bites to the limbs. It also lessens the pain from such contact because a numbness and coldness develops as a result of constricted blood supply.

5. The animal begins to sweat, drool, and secrete bodily fluids which, makes it slippery and difficult to grasp.

6. **Concentration** decreases while **attention** increases.

   Colloquially, we tend to use these two terms interchangeably; however, they are actually the opposite of one another. When one is concentrating, there is a sense of being focused on one stimulus: absorbed by one task. There is a limited awareness of extraneous stimuli that may distract from one's concentration. Attention is a state of hypervigilence: an increase in the sensitivity of the *radar system*. The animal quickly picks up movements, sounds, smells, etc. The ability to focus on one stimulus is diminished because the animal is attending to a variety of potential warning signals.

7. Muscle tone is enhanced; there is a muscle tension and a heightened state of arousal. The animal is poised for action.

You may be wondering why I have gone through this rather graphic scenario. It is an example of what occurs as a function of the fight or flight response as an organism prepares to protect itself. It is also what happens for humans on a regular basis day in and day out. **These also are** the symptoms of an anxiety attack (see **Figure 1**).

INCREASED HEART RATE
HYPERVENTILATION OR SHORTNESS OF BREATH
UPSET STOMACH
INCREASED PERSPIRATION
FEELING NUMB OR COLD IN THE FINGERS/HANDS
FEELING MUSCLE TENSION, "UPTIGHT"
DIFFICULTY CONCENTRATING

Figure 1. Symptoms of the fight or flight response.

The preceding symptoms are what lead to ulcers, hypertension, headaches, muscle tension, and fatigue and a variety of other stress-related illness. The following is a quote from Lawrence and Lawrence in *Nursing Forum*, #2, 1987-88, Vol. 23, pp. 45-51, that describes some of the process in physiological detail:

> Initially there is a sympathetic alarm response with intense vaso-constriction due to increased catecholamines. Anger causes a greater increase in norepinephrine than in epinephrine, possibly resulting in palpitations because of increased heart rate and the force of contractions. Vascular headaches may develop as a result of high blood pressure.
>
> There may be an elevated blood sugar as an adaptive response to meet the increased energy needs.
>
> Since stress is primarily psycho-cognitive in origin, the excess blood sugar may not be utilized and may trigger the secretion of an excess amount of insulin which causes stress hypoglycemia. This over time causes fatigue, nervousness, irritability and motor agitation.

STRESS IN LIFE

Hans Selye (1978), considered the Pioneer of Stress, has researched and written extensively on the subject. The following is information gathered from his book entitled, *The Stress of Life*.

Stress is a by-product of change. Stress is caused whenever a demand is placed upon us, be it a **physical, emotional or mental** event in our lives. **Figure 2** is a schematic representation of the impact of stress.

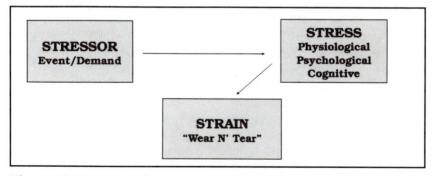

Figure 2. Diagram of stressor, stress, and strain.

A **stressor** is any event that places a demand upon the human organism. Over time, **stress** will develop as a result of this demand and will lead to a psychological and physiological response, usually precipitating a fight or flight response. If this stress is not resolved, **strain**, the wear and tear of unresolved stress, will develop.

Further, any stressor/event may be categorized as one of three types:

FRUSTRATION—The prevention of achieving a goal: one's needs not being met. This type of stress tends to be experienced as generating from an external source (i.e., a supervisor, spouse, etc.). An example is when an individual wishes to purchase an item, but his/her spouse says that they cannot afford it.

CONFLICT—Tension generated by incompatible inner needs or drives. It is derived from feelings within ourselves when we want to achieve two or more competing goals. This is often referred to as "role conflict." An example of role conflict would be the individual who would like to work overtime, but feels conflicted because it takes away from time with the family, or the supervisor who wants to be liked by his/her staff but must put pressure on them to work longer hours.

PRESSURE—The necessity or urgency of matters demanding immediate attention and needing to be accomplished rapidly and/or accurately.

Of course what is clear is that most stressors/events provide us with a combination of all three types of stress in varying proportionality.

In my workshops, I often conduct a demonstration in which I ask a man in the audience to volunteer as a subject. When the man approaches the front of the room, I ask his name, where he works, if he is married, has kids, etc. I then tell him to relax. Telling someone to relax while he is standing in front of a large audience not knowing what is to be expected is an example of an emotional stressor: receiving two conflicting and mixed messages. Further, **telling** someone to relax automatically makes it a **command** and, therefore, a **demand** and, hence, a **stressor**. I then proceed to drape my arm over his shoulders and lean on him with about 30 to 40 pounds of pressure. I have now generated a physical stressor in combination with the emotional stressor(s). I then ask the audience to describe what they witness the individual doing in response to my stressors; they usually report that the individual makes bodily movements in order to accommodate my weight. Often this bodily change is accompanied by a change of facial expression indicating either annoyance, humor, embarrassment, or a variety of other emotions. As an example of **strain**, I ask the audience to describe what they think would happen if we were to stay like this for about two hours. To further develop the demonstration, I ask them to imagine that I am a woman leaning on the subject. Further, instead of being in front of an audience in a brightly lit auditorium, imagine that we are now in a dimly lit lounge. And further yet, imagine that he is single... or married... or that his wife is across the room.

The purpose of this part of the performance is to demonstrate that what may be stressful to one person may be experienced very differently by another individual who has had different life experiences.

Remember, stress is not just an event but more importantly one's <u>perception</u> of and <u>associations</u> to the event.

Estimates are that at any given time approximately 15% to 20% of the work force is undergoing enough personal stress in their lives that it may impact upon their job performance. For any individual, the estimate is that once every seven years an accumulation of natural, significant life events may occur that may deeply affect him/her: births, deaths, marriages, marital problems, aging/ill parents, problematic children, work stress, money concerns, health issues. These are just a few of the many items on the *stress menu* that potentially may impair one's personal life and/or job performance.

These are all natural life events, most of which cannot be avoided. When we think of our physical and emotional selves, it is similar to buying a car. No matter how shiny and new the car is when it leaves the showroom, there is no way to avoid all the dents, scratches, squeaks, and rust spots that will develop over the course of normal usage.

The general agreement among most health professionals is that stress leads to physical problems. The estimate is that close to 60% of visits to physicians are precipitated by stress-related conditions. This is not to say that "it is all in his/her head"; rather, the physical conditions are legitimate medical problems that have been exacerbated by unresolved stress.

Experts agree that stress is cumulative; an individual may be unaffected for years, but the stress gradually builds until it starts to take its toll in any number of ways. "Diseases of adaptation" are not the direct result of an external agent but rather the consequence of the body's imperfect attempt to adapt to the wide variety of stressors. All of us come into this world with some component of our body that is more vulnerable than others to the effects of stress. For some it is an organ of the gastrointestinal tract and stress may result in ulcers, colitis, or spastic colon. For others it may be the respiratory system with impairments such as asthma. For still others it may be that the blood vessels in the cranium are arranged in such a way that stress leads to headaches. Some people manifest the effects of stress as emotional difficulties. The stress impacts upon neurotransmitter and hormonal production, leading to anxiety, depression, and anger. It behooves all of us to recognize that all parts of our body/mind are not built with equal quality control and that the human organism has a vast repertoire by which to manifest the effects of stress. Quite simply, if the human body were an automobile, all of us would be subject to the lemon law and at least a couple of *callback* orders.

STRESS MANAGEMENT

As most of you know, we have many coping mechanisms with which we deal with stress. However, many of these methods are negative and may relieve stress in the short run but, in fact, cause an increase of stress in the long run. Many people rely on eating, drinking, smoking, and other habits to relieve stress. Whenever I give presentations, I often am asked what can be done to cope with stress. Often people really want to know, "How can I get rid of the stress in my life?" I explain that the answer is simple: "You can't get rid of the stress in your lives." What *can* be done is to improve the body's and mind's capacity to resolve and mediate the impact of the stress. The methods to achieve this goal are really quite simple and involve three basic actions:

1. develop an objective understanding of the sources of stress,

2. improve one's physical and emotional tolerance for coping with the stress, and

3. make life-style modifications.

The first step toward stress management is defining the source of the stress: breaking it down into as small components as possible. For example, an individual may say: "I hate my job." When we are under stress we tend to overgeneralize. What would be recommended to this individual is to step back and look objectively at the job and determine what components are causing difficulties. Is it a **programmatic** problem... a **people/personnel** problem... a **personal problem**... or a **performance** problem.

> *Programmatic problem*—refers to the way that the job is designed. Often this type of problem may result when two jobs are being merged into one. Or there is a change in the job description.

> *People/personnel problem*—refers to personality conflicts and/or lack of personnel to manage the work load.

Personal problem—refers to issues outside of work that may be impacting on job performance (i.e., marital problem, illness, family issues).

Performance problem—refers to difficulty in performing job responsibilities. This may be as a result of aging in a job that requires physical strength. Or, the job requires further education/training for new equipment.

The second step toward stress management is to improve the tolerance of the mind and body. Efforts should be made to maintain a good "mindset" or develop PMA (positive mental attitude). When we are under stress we tend to become very negative, feel victimized, and allow the negativity to build and breed until we have made many mountains out of molehills. We then tend to look for others who share our view and unconsciously participate in the development of an epidemic. Avoidance of playing the *blame game* is essential. Developing a sense of self-acceptance of strengths, weaknesses, failures, and successes is essential. Find someone with whom you can speak easily: a spouse, friend, colleague, clergy, therapist. Develop new hobbies and activities as a method to renew interest in life. Joining a club, starting a new sport or hobby, taking music/dance lessons, doing volunteer work, joining a community theater group, or enrolling in an adult education course are a few of the "mental calisthenics" that one may do to improve the mental muscles.

Our body is a machine that can take quite a bit of abuse. However, many of us make little effort to keep ourselves in good physical condition. Put simply, the stress is not likely to go away. The only thing that we can do is to take better care of our bodies and minds so that when stress does hit, we are able to manage it. It may be helpful to use the metaphor of an athlete who sustains an injury. At some point in the performance of his/her job, too much stress was placed upon a vulnerable part of the body, resulting in a stress-related injury. Efforts are made to de-stress the symptom area and then gradually to exercise and strengthen the vulnerable area. Sometimes a major intervention (surgery) is required. The individual then must slowly build up the vulnerable area. The athlete does not expect that the game is going to get less stressful, but rather he/she now must learn to cope with the stress using different methods. Once an area of vulnerability has been injured, the athlete must devote time and energy to protecting and strengthening this area. Certainly, not all of us are professional athletes and able to take time off from the stress of our lives to heal. However, this example does serve as a concretization of the goals of the healing process.

In recent years, a great deal of "motivational literature" has been available in bookstores. *Unlimited Power* (Robbins, 1986), The Seven Habits of Highly Effective People (Covey,1990), *In Search of Excellence* (Peters & Waterman, 1988), *The One Minute Manager* (Blanchard & Johnson, 1982), and *Top Performance* (Zigler, 1987), are a few of the best known. I recommend that people wishing to improve their stress management skills read any of them. The focus of most of these publications is to assist us in moving from a reactive, victimized position to a more proactive, healthy attitude. These books promote our struggle against the natural tendency to look for the easy answers to come from outside ourselves when we all have the capacity to generate valuable resources and energy from within.

Thus, the key to stress management is harnessing, utilizing, and improving our own inner strengths and potential.

Chapter 2

CRITICAL INCIDENT STRESS (CIS)

In recent years, a large body of clinical research has developed with respect to trauma, crisis intervention, and disaster management. To facilitate effective use of this manual, consistent terminology will be used, and a working definition of each term will be helpful. With the use of each new term will be given an explanation of its meaning.

CRISIS, TRAUMA, DISASTER

Crisis

Crisis is an interruption from a previously normal state of functioning resulting in turmoil, instability, and significant upheaval in a system. A crisis may be physical as in a disease or maturational stage, emotional as in a mental disorder, social as in a geographic move or loss of a relationship, or professional as in the case of a layoff or termination.

Trauma

Trauma is an injury to living tissue caused by an extrinsic (outside) source. It may be the result of surgery, an act of violence, a natural disaster, etc. A trauma usually results in a state of crisis.*

Disaster

Disaster is a crisis in which traumatic injury and/or death has occurred to many people and often is accompanied by the destruction of property. Fires, transportation accidents, and natural events (hurricanes, earthquakes, etc.) are usually responsible for disasters.

UNDERSTANDING CRITICAL INCIDENT STRESS (CIS)

Much of the credit for the pioneer work that brought the term *Critical Incident Stress* to the public eye belongs to psychologist Dr. Jeffrey Mitchell while he was working at the University of Maryland. The terms *Critical Incident (CI)* and *Critical Incident Stress (CIS)* developed primarily as a result of his work with fire and police departments. These terms relate specifically to the impact of providing interventions to victims of trauma that is part and parcel of the duties of the Emergency Service Professional (ESP).

The primary purpose of this manual is to expand upon the work of Dr. Mitchell; to elaborate beyond the concept of CIS as it applies to police and fire departments, hospitals and ambulance services; and to recognize that various people in a multitude of roles may need to work with others who have experienced Critical Incident Stress and/or Trauma (CIS/T). Of equal importance, the intent of this manual is to examine the effects of trauma in the workplace and other places where persons experience trauma and crisis. As a point of embarkment, we will focus on CIS in its original scope: the response

---

*Note: Trauma is used in a specific context. Certainly, there are traumatic events and emotional traumas; however, in this manual it is being used in a clinical/physical context. This is not meant to imply that other uses of this term are incorrect.

of an ESP to the crises, trauma, and disasters with which they must deal in the performance of their jobs. Generally, it is understood that during an ESP's career, they will intervene with individuals experiencing crises and trauma. To some extent these events are considered "part of the job." Nonetheless, the effect of a career of this type has far-reaching impact.

The term *"trauma in the workplace"* is reserved for those events in which an industrial accident, personal injury/illness, or crime takes place in a work setting. Thus, employees may be victims or witnesses to an unexpected crisis. Whereas a police officer may expect to intervene with victims of trauma, a factory worker does not include this experience as part of his/her "job description."

Definition

A *Critical Incident (CI)* may be defined as an event that is extraordinary and produces significant reactions for the intervening person/ESP. It may be so unusual that it overwhelms the natural abilities that people have to cope with difficult situations. *Critical Incident Stress (CIS)* is often the natural reaction of a normal person to an extremely abnormal situation. (In this manual, **CIS** is sometimes referred to as **CIS/T**, *Critical Incident Stress/Trauma*.) It may manifest itself as a physical, cognitive, and/or emotional response that may be experienced almost immediately or may be delayed days, weeks, or months.

Release

Most ESP's manage the extreme stress of their careers quite well. Experience has documented that people who (1) understand the effects of CIS and (2) have an outlet and method by which to process their reactions, often speed up the recovery process, stay healthier, remain more productive on the job, and have less disruption in their home lives.

Multi-casualty

According to Mitchell, when most people refer to critical incidents, they automatically think of multi-casualty, catastrophic disasters such as earthquakes, plane crashes, train wrecks, etc. These are truly devastating events of monstrous proportions in which multiple trauma, loss of life, and significant destruction occur. However, large disasters usually generate an outpouring of community, if not national, support. Having a CI receive national or even regional media coverage is a statement that identifies that this incident is certainly unique and above and beyond the usual. The public acknowledgement is often experienced as a message to ESPs that it is alright if they have reactions to the incident. Often an entire community will bond together as a result of a multi-casualty disaster. In the process, an ESP will have a greater opportunity to process his/her reactions to the trauma. Further, during large incidents, personnel from other regions are often involved; or the National Guard or Red Cross may be activated to help with some major disasters.

Single Victim Incident

Mitchell pointed out that often the **single victim incident** is what may be most difficult for the intervening ESP. In **Figure 3** are listed the types of single victim incidents in order of severity for the ESP.

Line of duty death of fellow professional
Death of a child
Serious injury to a child
Death of an adult (dependent upon circumstances)
Threat of violence and/or personal injury to the ESP
Inability to intervene or perform duties
Injury to fellow ESPs
Suicide

Figure 3. Single victim incidents for emergency service professionals (listed in approximate order of severity).

In the case of the single victim incident, often the consideration is "business as usual." As a police officer said at one of my workshops, "If we had a debriefing after each of these events, we wouldn't have much time left to do our job." Most

ESPs conduct their own informal debriefings in the cruiser, back at the station, after work, in the nurses station, etc. As will be discussed later in this manual, it is imperative that each department has a policy that determines, among other things, when and under what circumstances a formal debriefing needs to be held. Depending upon the size and activity level of the department, different criteria may exist from one municipality or hospital to another.

Signs and Symptoms

CIS develops from a variety of incidents and may manifest itself in a myriad of different reactions. In **Figure 4** are listed signs and symptoms of Critical Incident Stress (CIS). It should be noted that they are similar to the *fight or flight response* previously described in Chapter 1. Further, the onset of the reaction may be experienced immediately during the incident or, as is usually the case, delayed by hours, days, or even weeks and months. Remember that at times of crisis, humans often experience a sense of detachment from the emotional impact of an event. This is an unconsciously activated protective mechanism that allows people to function in the face of extreme adversity. When speaking with ESPs, many describe experiencing an *autopilot* reaction when at the scene; they perform their duties with a sense of detachment and disconnection. They go on to describe becoming aware of symptoms and reactions after the *autopilot* reaction has diminished. If a debriefing immediately occurs following an incident, some ESPs may still be in *autopilot* mode and should be made aware of this natural response. They also should be warned about the possibility of delayed reactions.

As mentioned, the symptoms of CIS are similar to those of anxiety and panic disorders. However, one symptom is clearly unique to CIS and/or Post-traumatic Stress Disorder (see Chapter 4, Post-traumatic Stress Disorder): **intrusive thoughts and visions.** Many ESPs often report having some component of a critical incident continue to replay in their minds like a videotape. For others, it may be a thought or concern about their performance that continues to "loop" through their mind without resolution. Although these are considered typical reactions to CIS, they may be a disturbing and disruptive experience interfering with sleep, work, and personal relations. At times, individuals resort to alcohol and/or drugs/medication as a way of coping with these reactions.

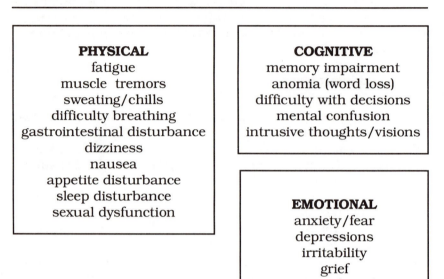

PHYSICAL
fatigue
muscle tremors
sweating/chills
difficulty breathing
gastrointestinal disturbance
dizziness
nausea
appetite disturbance
sleep disturbance
sexual dysfunction

COGNITIVE
memory impairment
anomia (word loss)
difficulty with decisions
mental confusion
intrusive thoughts/visions

EMOTIONAL
anxiety/fear
depressions
irritability
grief
remoteness/numbness
intrusive thoughts/visions

Figure 4. Signs and symptoms of Critical Incident Stress.

Defense Mechanisms

People working in "at risk" professions (See Chapter 3: Description of "At Risk" Occupations) develop a variety of defense mechanism by which they manage the emotional impact of their careers. I refer to these as ***"emotional callouses."*** Callouses serve a useful purpose. A callous forms over a portion of sensitive skin, making that area tough and less sensitive to contact with rough tools, hardened surfaces, or physical labor. As we all know, a callous on the hand is not like a work glove, something that may be removed when we are done with a job. In fact, the callous stays long after we have discontinued the activity through which the callous developed. People may develop emotional callouses in much the same manner and for the same purpose. The emotional callous may be protective, but it also may promote insensitivity. One example that seems to permeate most police and fire departments, hospitals, residential psychiatric settings, and military bases is a "weird" sense of humor. It is a humor that helps individuals deal with the difficult areas of their work and bonds them together, but it easily does not transfer to the "real world."

Using the sense of humor as an example of "emotional callousness" is not to suggest that it is inappropriate. Actually humor is considered a high-level defense. The problem is that it may serve to protect the individual but be experienced as insensitive or inappropriate by others.

REACTION AND TIME DELAY

At this point, we are discussing CIS as it relates to the Emergency Services Professional. However, crises and trauma happen to individuals, organizations, and communities. Remember that in a critical incident you have the victim and the ESP, both of whom may have an emotional reaction as a result of the incident. The following describes the types of reactions with respect to time delay. It should be noted that the closer to the event one experiences the reactions, the easier is the resolution.

Acute

The acute response is recognized easily by the individual and/or observing colleagues as it impacts almost immediately in relation to the event. Some people report having a reaction at the scene that interferes with their ability to perform their duties. Often these individuals experience feelings of guilt, humiliation, and inadequacy as a result of their impaired performance. It is essential that these individuals receive immediate debriefing around the event in order to avoid the possible risk of further impairment. Most often a 12-to 24-hour delay occurs as the individual transitions out of autopilot. This is similar to performing a strenuous athletic event; we do not feel the muscle strain until the next day, after a period of rest. In the case of an acute reaction, the symptoms are usually obvious to the individual as well as others and may be experienced with dramatic intensity.

Delayed

The delayed reaction may manifest itself rather suddenly between 72 hours and some extended period of time after the event. Prior to this, the individual may be void of any feelings or reactions connected to the incident. The CIS symptoms may be triggered by some seemingly minor and/or unrelated incident. However, on a conscious or unconscious level, the "unrelated incident" triggers associations of the event. An example of this was described by one fire fighter who had a child fatality in a house fire. He seemed to handle this situation well until several weeks later when responding to a small incident in which a child had sustained a minimal injury. After the incident, he had what he described as an *overreaction* and could not understand why he was so troubled by such a minor accident. In discussing it further, he realized that this "child-incident" had triggered a delayed CIS response to the incident in which a child had died.

Cumulative or Gradual CIS

Cumulative or gradual CIS is often referred to as **burnout.** It is much more serious and has longer and more permanent effects. It is often more difficult to resolve as it is not attached to any one single traumatic incident, but rather it is an accumulation of *emotional sludge* that has built up over time. It is usually a gradual and insidious process in which the **burnout** has impacted upon many aspects of the individual's life. To determine what is "job stress" from "personal stress" is most difficult. An ESP experiencing serious burnout may be subject to a variety of somatic symptoms and illnesses. In many cases, alcohol and/or drugs are being used to excess by the individual as a way of coping with cumulative stress. In **Figure 5** is a summary of the stages leading to burnout as reported by Mitchell and Resnik (1981) in *Emergency Response to Crisis.*

STAGE 1— Early Warning Signs
vague anxiety
fatigue
feelings of depression
apathy
moderate social isolation

STAGE 2— Mild Burnout
lowered emotional control
increased anxiety
sleep disturbance
headaches
diffuse physical symptoms
irritability

STAGE 3— Moderate Burnout
skin rashes
generalized physical weakness
strong feelings of depression
increased blood pressure
increased alchohol/drug usage
loss of appetite
loss of sexual desire
emotional outbursts
development of irrational fears (phobias)
difficulty with interpersonal relationships
ulcers or other GI distress

STAGE 4— Serious Burnout
serious medical conditions
severe withdrawal
emotional lability
accident proneness
severe depression
suicidal thoughts/actions
serious psychiatric disorders

Figure 5. Outline of stages leading to burnout (gradual Critical Incident Stress).

In Chapter 3, Description of "At Risk" Occupations, is an explanation of the type of person predisposed to developing **burnout**.

Chapter **3**

DESCRIPTION OF "AT RISK" OCCUPATIONS

The types of employment that qualify as "*at risk*" are probably obvious. An at risk occupation may be defined loosely as an employment that has the potential of placing professionals in critical incidents and thus with the possibility of experiencing varying degrees of CIS. As has been discussed previously in this manual, most notable are the Emergency Service Professions: police officers, fire fighters, ambulance services, nurses, crisis workers, and clergy. **These professions have as their primary objective the care of other human beings as a result of some kind of crisis.** Without question, being in the emergency service professions is a highly stressful career.

Emergency services has seen a significant change in current duties as compared to those of a generation ago. Increased population, larger buildings, synthetic materials, and hazardous materials ("haz mat") have made the fire service an altogether different occupation.

The ambulance service has moved from the "meat wagon" days to very sophisticated vehicles equipped with the latest medico-technical apparatus. The ambulance driver of yesterday is now an Emergency Medical Technician (EMT) or a paramedic with a significant amount of medical education, trained to deal with a wide diversity of trauma.

A similar evolution has taken place for police departments as they battle more sophisticated criminals with greater firepower. Also, they must face greater amounts of bureaucratic red tape in the execution of their duties.

For the ESP, the job requires that a small group of people must respond without much advanced notice to experiences that may be life-and-death situations. They must make quick decisions with limited information, often under adverse physical and emotional conditions. The job of anticipating emergency situations creates a constant state of stress. In the book, *People Under Pressure*, Dr. Albert Barnett (1960) described this for fire fighters as "expectancy pressure." Although ESP learns to handle these pressures and perform his/her duties, the pressures are always present and causing stress.

EFFECTS OF STRESS

In the mid-1970s, the U.S. Department of Health Education and Welfare (HEW) began to take a look at the stress for police officers. These studies reported that police officers have an increased vulnerability to

cardiovascular disease,

other stress-related disorders,

divorce (The divorce rate is nearly two times higher for police personnel than other professionals.),

alcoholism (A National Police Foundation study reported that 23% of police officers have an alcohol problem; 10% reported drug problem.), and

suicide (The rate for police personnel is higher than many other professionals.).

Other studies began to show the same results. Police have a higher rate of heart attacks, premature death, and physiological disorders. Similar studies have been conducted with fire service personnel yielding similar results.

The level of stress among hospital workers has increased over the past two decades due to advances in medical technology. There is "an emphasis on accountability and efficiency and by pressure to improve the quality of patient care despite limited resources. Patients are being discharged earlier and staff-to-patient ratios are dropping. As a result, caregivers are not producing what they perceive as high quality care." (Cerne, *Hospitals*, 10/5/88). Although all aspects of nursing are difficult because nurses deal with people who are ill, incapacitated, vulnerable, and regressed, in certain areas within a hospital setting the stress may be considered to be greater. Certainly acute settings such as the emergency department, operating room, and pediatric unit are at the top of the list, followed closely by oncology and psychiatry. Chronic care settings are certainly stressful and develop a unique type of stress; however, crisis is not as sudden in chronic care settings and there is an expectation that develops in these types of settings.

FACTORS AFFECTING RISK

Several factors help to determine and identify the level of risk that a job may hold. These are summarized under seven headings with all words beginning with "I."

Intervention

Jobs that require intervention with people in crisis cause stress. Whenever a profession requires the provision of services to people in crisis, one may expect stress. The expectation is that these professionals will do something to alleviate the crisis. This is a different type of stress from that of an engineer who has to build a computer by a deadline or a salesperson who must meet a certain quota. Certainly these jobs are stressful, however a different quality is necessitated when one's provision of services involves other people in crisis.

Immediacy

A factor in stress is the time pressure involved in performing the interventions. Must the individual work quickly in the performance of his/her duties? ESPs often describe their concern about the time element involved with their crisis work. Often a distortion of time and activities is experienced with things moving rapidly or seeming to take forever. Concern over accuracy and quality of interventions usually goes along with the concern over time.

Intensity

Another stress factor is the level of the crisis, the duration, and the frequency of interventions that are being performed. What is the nature of the intervention? How many casualties? What type of casualties? What types of victims are involved in this crisis? How long must ESPs function in their capacity? How often is the department/individual/agency involved in these types of activities?

Instability

The level of physical and/or emotional risk to the victim causes an instability, which produces stress. As difficult as it is to arrive at an accident scene to obvious fatalities, sometimes a more stressful situation is to have a victim alive but in a critically unstable condition. This places all of the aforementioned factors in action. Arriving on the scene to fatalities may be extremely painful; however, the *Intensity* and *Immediacy* of the situation may be diminished.

Information

The amount of (or often expressed as lack of) data and other information that ESPs have about the situation to which they are responding causes stress. During a crisis, information is so important ESPs start to prepare intellectually and protect emotionally themselves.

Imperilment

The level of or potential danger involved for the caregiver can be very stressful. Can the intervening professional be hurt as a result of performing his/her duties? This concept may be further divided into two distinct areas:

Acute concerns—Injury as a result of activities at the scene of an incident, getting hurt in a fire, responding to a robbery, etc.

Long-term concerns—Potential illnesses that may result through infection, contact with contaminated blood, inhalation of toxic fumes, and/or contact with hazardous waste materials ("haz mat").

Isolation

Performing an intervention by one's self or with one other individual (partner) increases the level of stress, as does being at the scene with a limited number of personnel available to assist with the crisis. Oftentimes, a police officer may be the first at the scene of an accident. Because police officers frequently patrol alone and often have limited medical training and no proper medical equipment, they may be left in a helpless position with respect to intervening with the victim. EMTs who have the training and equipment often feel a sense of insecurity, increased stress and isolation when *on the street.* In comparison, an emergency room has much trauma, but there is a safe feeling knowing that one is within a hospital, with other personnel, with plenty of equipment, and bright lights. The environment is relatively safe and familiar as compared to the chaotic and unfamiliar scene of an accident.

Public Approval

At this point, it is important to mention another factor involved in determining the level of risk for a profession. What is the level of public approval/esteem of the job? During the past two decades police and fire service personnel have received a great deal of public degradation. The public has little to no memory of positive actions on the part of the public safety officer but will call for immediate action if there is a questionable situation.

CHARACTERISTICS OF INDIVIDUALS
IN HELPING PROFESSIONS

The reactions to a Critical Incident may vary a great deal depending upon the nature of the CI as well as on the character of the individual involved as victim or ESP. Over the years, various studies have been made to explore what types of individuals choose different professions. The characteristics identified in people choosing the emergency services (police officers, fire fighter, EMT, paramedic, nurse) are provided in **Figure 6**.

ESPs tend to

> **prefer to be active**
> **enjoy challenges**
> **need to feel valued, appreciated, important**
> **try to please others in authority positions***
> **try to control their emotions**
> **have strong rescuer motivations**
> **prefer to be the "helper" rather than the "helpee"**
> (they do not make great patients)
> **be excellent in a crisis and able to take charge**

*Note: They will attempt to please authority figures up to a certain point. If they are not successful with their efforts, they may tend to become resentful and very negative with respect to those individuals.

Figure 6. Characteristics identified in people who choose the emergency services.

At one of my conferences, a veteran police officer described police and fire personnel as "dog personalities." He went on to describe that they are loyal, can take a fair amount of abuse, and respond well to the occasional pat on the head. At first blush this seemed a rather self-deprecating and disrespectful analysis. However, it drew a murmur of approval from other ESPs in the room.

Another commonly reported characteristic among people choosing the "helping professions" is that an inordinate number come from "dysfunctional families". I assume that anyone reading this manual has a basic understanding of the terms *dysfunctional family, co-dependency, adult-child.* Stated simply, a *dysfunctional family* is a family unit in which one (or more) of the parents are alcoholic/drug addicted or impaired in some other fashion. The impairment prevents the individual(s) from functioning as an adequate parent; thus, the child often grows up in an environment in which he/she may (1) not receive adequate nurturance and guidance, (2) have to take on adult responsibilities (e.g., take care of other children), (3) witness a wide variety of emotional and physical crises, and (4) often assume a caretaking role with either the impaired parent or the **co-dependent** parent. The term co-dependent is used to describe the other partner in the couple whose life is so entwined with and affected by the impaired individual that they too are considered impaired. A myriad of books and articles is available on this subject, and I would recommend that people become familiar with the characteristics of adults who have grown up in dysfunctional families. Certain personality characteristics predispose some ESPs to burnout. In the book, *Burn-out*, H. Freudenberger (1980) identified the following personality types most prone to developing symptoms of burnout:

1. the overcommitted staff member whose home life is unsatisfactory (to this person, work is a substitute for social life);

2. the authoritarian worker who relies on authority and obedience to control others;

3. the overworked administrator who begins to view himself/herself as indispensable; and/or

4. the professional who tends to overidentify with those with whom he/she is working.

People in *at risk* professions should be aware of the possible negative impact of their job and should take precautions. Fire service professionals are trained to handle hazardous materials in a certain manner. Emergency room staff are instructed to take precautions when treating patients who may be HIV positive.

Similarly, people working in **at risk** professions must be trained to protect themselves from the potential of the emotional risks involved. Heads of emergency service departments must understand the need for Employee Assistance Programs, stress units, debriefings, and training on the issue of CIS.

I am including a letter that I received from a police officer who was involved in a very difficult incident in which a mother was killed in front of her two children. The police officer was involved in the original crime scene, the apprehension of the suspect (at gunpoint), and the hospital emergency room with the children. Letters like this one communicate the true intensity of the experience and the benefit of intervention.

I am writing this letter in behalf of myself and my family. I first was introduced to you almost two years ago at a union meeting. I was impressed by your presentation and by the fact that the city was caring enough to have a counseling program for stress within the police department.

Shortly there after I was involved in a homicide that involved an entire family. Due to the fact that my Chief and supervisor were concerned I was introduced to the meaning of critical stress incidents.

You came to the police station and began to deprogram the entire midnight shift, firemen and paramedics. I can't begin to tell you how important you were that day. I was in shock and did not even know it. The course of events of that day has stayed with me until this day. Viewing the deceased mother, arresting the husband and then returning to the scene to take care of the children still is painful to recall.

On that morning you talked with us, comforted us and you let us know it was ok to feel what we were feeling.

I also appreciate the follow-up calls and visits that you made. Without this program many police officers would have to deal with these critical stress incidents alone. For many years as a police officer I had to deal with this alone. It drove me crazy. Over 10 suicides and many fatal accidents without no counseling or advice. The worst was an 8 year old boy that died in my arms in front of his mother. Just imagine getting out of work at 8:00am and having to be normal with your children after being involved with such a violent incident. I need you to know you as a psychologist have helped me and many others through some bad times.

I am living proof that if you look for help in this law enforcement profession you will find it. I think that the law enforcement profession has accepted the new attitude and what the consequences are to being exposed to excessive danger, split-second decisions and human misery on a daily basis.

I also want to thank you and the city for having your services available to our families. Sometimes CSI will affect police officers and their families. Thank you for your patience and common sense approach to help me and my family through a tough time. You showed my wife things that she did not know about stress in law enforcement on a daily basis. You did make a difference in my life. I hope that the city retains your services especially since you have been developing a rapport with all of the officers. It was not too long ago police officers would do everything to hide the fact that they needed help. I think this has changed because of your time and the effort of the city and its leaders.

P.S. If I can be of any assistance to you in reference to speaking to police officers that need assistance or going to other departments to speak, please feel free to call at any time.

Letters like this one do not cross one's desk on a regular basis, but when they do, they are a gift.

Chapter **4**

POST-TRAUMATIC STRESS DISORDER (PTSD)

For many years, a common recognition has been that during warfare soldiers may develop a stress response to the combat experience. In the classic novel written by Stephen Crane in 1885, *The Red Badge of Courage*, the stress response of a civil war soldier is reported in vivid detail. Even ancient civilizations were aware of the reactions of warriors returning from battle and had rituals to help deal with the reactions (Crane, 1987). Freud (1957) used the experiences of World War I to develop his theory of depression as expressed through his writings in *Mourning and Melancholia.*

In modern times, we have assigned a number of terms to the reactions of combatants to warfare, and what we now call Post-traumatic Stress Disorder (PTSD) has been around under different names. During World War I soldiers experienced "*shell shock*." In World War II it was described as "*battle fatigue*." As we moved into the 50s and into psychology, soldiers in Korea were diagnosed as having "*combat neurosis*" and Vietnam vets received the label of *Post-traumatic Stress Disorder*.

DETERMINANTS OF PTSD

Whereas once the syndrome was viewed almost exclusively as a result of armed combat, now PTSD may result from a variety of noncombat related experiences as well. In more recent years, it has become a legitimate diagnosis that may be applied to a number of situations including

extreme combat situations,
victim/witness of a traumatic incident,
victim/witness of a violent crime,
victim/witness of physical mistreatment, and
victim/witness of sexual mistreatment.

Although it is not reported in the literature, I would add to this list *unresolved Critical Incident Stress*.

Figure 7 is an outline of the criteria of Post-traumatic Stress Disorder as described in the *Diagnostic and Statistical Manual of Mental Disorders, Third Edition, Revised* (APA, 1987).

To summarize, the key determinants of PTSD are

1. exposure to an extraordinary stressor outside the usual realm of human experience,

2. intrusive psychological reexperiencing of the traumatic event,

3. psychological numbing/avoidance of and involvement with the external environment,

4. autonomic nervous system hyperactivity and/or hyperfunction, and

5. the symptoms must last for at least one month.

A. The person has experienced an event that is outside the range of usual human experience and that would be markedly distressing to almost anyone, e.g., serious threat to one's life or physical integrity; serious threat or harm to one's children, spouse, or other close relatives and friends; sudden destruction of one's home or community; or seeing another person who has recently been, or is being, seriously injured or killed as the result of an accident or physical violence.

B. The traumatic event is persistently reexperienced in at least one of the following ways:

(1) recurrent and intrusive distressing recollections of the event
(2) recurrent distressing dreams of the event
(3) sudden acting or feeling as if the traumatic event were recurring (includes a sense of reliving the experience, illusions, hallucinations, and dissociative [flashback] episodes, even those that occur upon awakening or when intoxicated)
(4) intense psychological distress at exposure to events that symbolize or resemble an aspect of the traumatic event, including anniversaries of the trauma

C. Persistent avoidance of stimuli associated with the trauma or numbing of general responsiveness (not present before the trauma), as indicated by at least three of the following:

(1) efforts to avoid thoughts or feelings associated with the trauma
(2) efforts to avoid activities or situations that arouse recollections of the trauma
(3) inability to recall an important aspect of the trauma (psychogenic amnesia)
(4) markedly diminished interest in significant activities
(5) feeling of detachment or estrangement from others
(6) restricted range of affect, e.g., unable to have loving feelings
(7) sense of a foreshortened future, e.g., does not expect to have a career, marriage, or children, or a long life

D. Persistent symptoms of increased arousal (not present before the trauma), as indicated by at least two of the following:

(1) difficulty falling or staying asleep
(2) irritability or outbursts of anger
(3) difficulty concentrating
(4) hypervigilence
(5) exaggerated startle response
(6) physiologic reactivity upon exposure to events that symbolize or resemble an aspect of the traumatic event (e.g., a woman who was raped in an elevator breaks out in a sweat when entering any elevator)

E. Duration of the disturbance (symptoms in B, C, and D) of at least one month.

Specify delayed onset if the onset of symptoms was at least six months after the trauma.

Figure 7. Diagnostic criteria for post-traumatic stress disorder 309.89. Source: American Psychiatric Association (1987), *Diagnostic and statistical manual of mental disorders (Third Edition-Revised), p.250.* Reprinted with permission.

RELATIONSHIP OF CIS TO PTSD

If we compare the symptoms of Critical Incident Stress (CIS) and Post-traumatic Stress Disorder (PTSD) it seems that they describe a similar syndrome. It is important to note that CIS is not a clinical diagnosis but rather a neologism developed from work with police and fire personnel. Further, as indicated by the DSM-III-R criteria, PTSD should be assigned only to people who are symptomatic for *at least one month*. The goal of early intervention with ESPs is to resolve CIS before it results in a more serious diagnosis of PTSD.

In **Figure 8** is a schematic diagram of the relationship between CIS and PTSD as it involves the victim as well as the Emergency Service Professional. An incident may occur in which a person becomes the victim in an accident or violent crime. An ESP arrives at the scene and provides intervention to the victim. This interaction may in fact be an event/incident for the ESP and may result in the development of CIS. Therefore, both the *victim* and the *ESP* may experience symptoms as a result of the incident. Since PTSD should not be used as a diagnostic label unless the symptoms persist for more than one month, I recommend that neither the ESP nor the victim be labeled as such. Certainly, most victims of serious trauma remain symptomatic for a time period greater than one month and appropriately would be diagnosed with PTSD. However, with suitable intervention to the ESP, the development of PTSD and/or "burnout" may be diminished significantly. In the same way that one attempts to take care of a cold in order that it not develop into pneumonia, for the Emergency Service Professional, the goal of managing CIS is to avoid possible PTSD.

CASE EXAMPLES OF PTSD IN CLINICAL PRACTICE

As indicated, PTSD may result from a variety of overwhelming events. Often people will experience the impact of the crisis/trauma almost immediately, or it may be delayed by several months or even years. The following are two case examples of individuals with PTSD. One experienced her reaction within two weeks of the incident, the other was delayed more than 25 years. Although permission was given to include theses cases, efforts have been made to protect the identity of those individuals by changing names and some identifiable data.

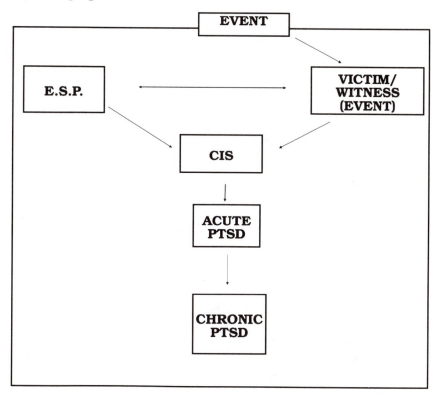

Figure 8. Schematic diagram of the relationship between Critical Incident Stress and Post-traumatic Stress Disorder.

Case 1

Mary is a 45-year-old, married mother of two children, ages 20 and 18. Both children are in college, living at school. Mary has worked as a paralegal for the past 10 years and enjoys her work very much. Her husband is a sales representative for a furniture company.

Mary and Dave were on vacation on a secluded island at a sprawling hotel resort comprised of separate guest suites. They were with another couple and decided to go to sleep early as they had been sight-seeing and out to dinner that evening. As they turned off the lights to the room, Mary was aware that it had begun to rain with much thunder and lightning.

In the early morning, predawn hours, two men broke into the room through a window, and Mary awoke to find the men screaming at them for their money. Awakened from a sound sleep, in a dark room, having lost his sense of where he was, Dave was disoriented and unable to find his wallet. With no notice, warning or reason, one of the men shot Dave and then both men ran out of the bungalow. Mary reported that at the time she felt very calm but remembered having the thought that she was going to die.

After the men fled, Mary reports that she remained calm, observing that there was much blood, but that Dave was conscious, lying on the floor propped against the foot of the bed. Dave, too, was calm. He had been a medic in Vietnam, was aware of his physical state, and was calmly describing his experience of feeling numb, going into shock, feeling light headed, etc.

The ambulance took 20 minutes to arrive at the hotel resort and Dave was taken to a *local* hospital, which was comprised of one small wooden building with open windows. Mary remembers seeing Dave lying on a table below one of these windows with the rain splashing in through the window on him. She was asked to leave and wandered outside. She was standing on the porch of this building, looking down into the harbor as the sun was rising and a cruise ship was pulling into the harbor. It was still raining and she remembers wondering to herself: "Are the people (on the ship) having fun?"

Plans were made to move Dave to a larger hospital on another island. Weather held up the transport, and when the plane did land and Dave was loaded on board, Mary was informed that she could not go because she did not have the appropriate passport. At this time, Dave was in critical condition and she did not know whether or not she would see him again. It had now been more than six hours since the shooting incident, and both she and Dave became very emotional when they had to be separated.

When Mary was able to get to the other island and find her way to the hospital, some six hours later, she was told a room number in which she could find Dave. When she went to that room, it was empty, and she was approached by a physician wanting to talk to her. She remembers being sure that Dave had died, and she was prepared to hear this from the physician. Instead, he informed her that Dave had been moved and that he was doing fine.

Dave remained in that hospital, and they flew home together about 10 days later. Mary did not become symptomatic until she returned home.

Mary was referred by her physician and she presented with the following symptoms:

1. She was unable to fall asleep unless the lights were on in the bedroom.

2. She had been experiencing episodic overactive, emotional outbursts. During one, she became extremely volatile toward the clerk at the grocery store, threatening to do bodily injury. (She had no previous history of violence.)

3. She experienced a fear of any kind of disagreement or confrontation.

4. She was avoiding people at work and having difficulty performing her usual duties.

5. She had a decrease in eating and subsequent weight loss.

6. She reported having "crazy dreams that don't make sense."

7. She also had anxiety reactions when it rained.

After Mary described the precipitant, I asked if she had been experiencing any intrusive thoughts, visions, or hallucinations. At first she hesitated, but then responded affirmatively. On rainy nights, if she looked out onto the street in front of her house, she would see the "cruise ship in the harbor." She also could produce this vision if she closed her eyes. Anther intrusive vision was seeing Dave bleeding on the floor.

Briefly, treatment consisted of the following:

1. Educating her about PTSD including giving her a copy of the print out from the DSM-III-R and other articles.

2. Using a variety of methods, including talking about the incident, viewing pictures from the vacation, etc. By so doing, we slowly *painted the picture* of what happened on the vacation. We focused on feelings of rage, guilt, shame, and abandonment.

3. Utilizing self-hypnosis for relaxation training.

4. Medicating by use of an antidepressant.

In general, I attempted to treat her as a *normal* person who had experienced an extremely difficult event and was experiencing a natural reaction. Within six months, the majority of Mary's symptoms were gone, and those that remained were diminished significantly.

Case 2

At the time I saw this patient, she was 45 years old. She had been referred by her physician because she had been experiencing a variety of vague somatic complaints, emotional lability, and difficulties in her relationship with her husband. She also had become a difficult patient to her physician who "could find nothing wrong with her."

When we met, she was verbal, cooperative, and sincere about wishing to feel better. She sensed that she was viewed by her physician as a difficult patient with many maladies that did not improve regardless of the treatment.

During my initial evaluation, which took about two sessions, I asked my standard questions about presenting problem(s), family history, drugs and/or alcohol in the family, physical and/or sexual mistreatment, etc. She reported that her father was an alcoholic and that he had been physically abusive to her; however, she denied sexual abuse.

At the next session, she came in obviously agitated because she had not told me "all of the truth." She then proceeded to report that she had been physically and sexually abused by her father from latency through adolescence. She made great efforts to suppress this from her conscious awareness and had been relatively successful until an incident had occurred the previous summer.

She went on to describe that she had been cooking in her kitchen and talking on the phone when her house was struck by lightning. The next thing she knew she was thrown across the room and landed on the floor at the end of the kitchen farthest from the phone with a significant head wound and much bleeding. She felt "numb and tingly" throughout her body and a pulsing sensation traveling up and down inside her. (It was later determined that the electrical current had traveled through the phone lines.)

She had a vague memory of being taken to the hospital, being treated, and being released all within the same day. She described feeling "weird," awkward, and emotionally uncomfortable for the next few days; her head was swimming and she had a hard time thinking clearly.

Her husband suggested that they go away for a few days to a little cottage in the mountains. While there, she remembers that her husband initiated sexual activity and that as he approached her, he was silhouetted in the small bedroom doorway by a lamp in the adjacent room. She began to feel anxious, but was willing to participate in what she hoped would be a romantic interlude. However, as her husband touched her she "freaked out totally" and was unable to continue the sexual activity then or for the remainder of the vacation. In fact, sex had become very difficult for her even upon returning from the trip.

As we worked together, she allowed the memories of being physically and sexually abused to surface. She reported that the feeling of being thrown across the room by the lightning was similar to a beating she had received from her father, complete with head wound and bleeding. The physical "numbness and tingly feeling" also was reminiscent of the feelings she had during the sexual abuse. When she saw her husband silhouetted in the small doorway, he appeared very large to her, and she had an **abreaction**—a momentary regression and reexperiencing of the original trauma—and actually felt that her husband was her father. Of course, this was all unclear to her at the time and very confusing. She began to develop a wide variety of psychosomatic symptoms and other psychological symptoms as her psyche tried to resolve the breach in the defense system generated by the lightning incident.

DYNAMICS INVOLVED WITH PTSD

PTSD is an extremely complicated and complex disorder that is receiving significant attention. The purpose of this book is not to delve deeply into this subject, but rather to define it as it relates to CIS and identify it as a reaction to trauma. (For those wishing to read a well written and comprehensive work on PTSD, *Trauma and Recovery* by Judith Herman (1992) is strongly recommended.) The aforementioned case study (Case 2) is an example of unresolved PTSD that was reactivated more than 20 years later by an incident that triggered unconsciously associated material. Although not totally **repressed**, this woman had been **suppressing** painful memories from her past. The trauma of the lightning and the image of her husband in the doorway weakened her emotional defensive system, and the painful material flushed to the surface. Many Vietnam veterans experience a similar type of abreaction or reexperiencing of an incident. These abreactive events are often referred to as "flashbacks"; they feel very real as if the person has been transported in time and space back to the original event. They are extremely disruptive and disorganizing to the individual, often producing concerns about "going crazy" or "losing it". Often some visual image becomes permanently imprinted in the mind of the individual. If something later in life sparks an association to the event, it is as if a tape recording is being replayed. The association may be some seemingly neutral occurrence that holds unconscious meaning to the individual. For Mary (Case 1), it was rain that could trigger massive feelings of anxiety as well as the hallucination of the cruise ship. A Vietnam veteran with whom I worked described mowing the lawn when the grass was very long because there had been several days of rain. The day he chose to cut the grass was very hot and humid. After cutting several swaths in the lawn he began to feel very anxious and uncomfortable, left the lawnmower idling, and ran in the house. Later, he was able to figure that the smell of the freshly cut grass on a hot humid day triggered olfactory associations of the jungles of Vietnam. Whether it be PTSD or CIS, these types of intrusive thoughts and visions, or associations to critical incidents and events, are often part of the symptom picture.

As more research is conducted, increasing evidence has become available indicating that involvement with trauma may have a dramatic effect on individuals. Manifestations may occur immediately or remain submerged within the unconscious for long periods of time. The individual may appear to be alright to others around him/her. However, this may be the beginning of the period of emotional adjustment, the "honeymoon" period. Or, it could be a defensive facade or mask that is used to hide the real inner turmoil, confusion, and pain. For many people who have experienced PTSD, the recovery period is often a minimum of two years.

Case 3

The following is an edited transcript of a therapy session with another patient. The patient was involved in a serious explosion that killed two people and injured others. He spent a month in the hospital recovering from his injuries. He experienced no emotional symptoms until his return home from the hospital. At that point he began to experience serious nightmares, intrusive thoughts and visions, anxiety, and depressive symptoms. As you read the transcript, be aware of the primary issue—loss of control: his description of going into shock (during the explosion) and remaining very lucid; his fixation on the other injured worker; the development of his emotional symptoms; and his anger at not being understood by others. As you read, please remember that this individual had not had an easy life and had been on his own since age 16. In his own words he said, "I've been beaten up, stabbed, rode bikes and am covered with tattoos."

We had been working together for some time when we reviewed the "accident" that had taken place more than a year prior to this interview.

What happened the day of the accident is something that I had absolutely no control over—which is the biggest problem I have. It was a major explosion that killed two people and put two people in the hospital. I was one of them. I had no idea it was coming; there was no indication it was going to happen. The only thing on my mind was my 10:00 break in five minutes. All of a sudden my world came to an end.

What were you doing, exactly, Bob? Try to describe specifically what occurred.

Well I had my back turned to the explosion. I was doing my regular daily job... and the lights went out. I didn't realize what happened for a few minutes later. I thought that I never went unconscious, but obviously there are moments I don't remember. So whether it was just a blackout or I went unconscious. Now, some how I got on the floor. All of a sudden there was instant pain... Beyond belief. The flesh was melting off my body, I could feel it.

But some how you managed to get yourself up. What did you do?

I think the sprinklers put me into shock or something, cause I didn't feel any pain after that. And at that point that's when I actually started to think what was going on. The only thing that I realized was that I was burning alive, literally...and there was nothing I could do about it.

Were you scared, were you calm? What were your reactions?

I thought I was going to die.

You had that actual thought...?

After the sprinklers came on, I was very, very rational. I wasn't scared, I thought about where I was...

You told me that it was dark...

It was so dark, it has never been that dark in my life. Even in a pitch dark room. I didn't know if my eyes had burned shut or what happened. All I know was that I couldn't see anything, it was total blackness. I think the only reason I got out of there anyways is cause I had been there so long. It was probably one of the most rational moments of my life was right then.

(transition)

What was the time frame? How long did all of this seem to be?

I found out later that it was a total of 12 minutes. It seemed like a lot longer than that.

From when to when?

From the explosion to when I walked out. I was one of the last ones out.

How long did it seem?

Days, days... it seemed it never ended in your mind. The pain went on.

(transition)

Say a little more about your experience in the ambulance...

God, it was disgusting. His ears were burned off, he was totally black. He had no lips... the whitest teeth I ever saw. His eyes were burned closed. He had no idea of what was happening to him or why. Nothing I could do but stand there looking at him. They should never have put him in the ambulance with me. God, that haunted me for months.

Seeing him?

Over and over and over again. It was the most horrible thing I've ever seen in my life.

And he talked to you? He asked you if he was ok?

He didn't know what happened to him. He had no idea what happened. He went into a coma and never came out of it afterward. You never seen teeth as white as his. He had no lips.They were burned off. His face was totally charred. It was like a dead piece of wood you pull out of the fire. It wasn't even blistered... just charcoal black.

You kept having sort of visions or dreams of that...

For months and months.

When you were sleeping or when you were awake?

Both. It was weird. A lot of the times it just popped into my head. I'd be watching TV, it'd pop into my head. Whatever. I'd wake up screaming.

(transition)

Can you speak to the emotional side...

Its all kind of numb...   the whole experience in the hospital. I mean I had absolutely no control of my life. My hands were in plastic cases, all bandaged up, I couldn't do nothing. I couldn't wash my own hair and there were a few other things I couldn't do either.

You were really very helpless.

I was totally helpless like a newborn baby. I was totally helpless. It really made me feel inadequate as a human being.

Could that have been avoided... or that was just the way it went?

That just was the way it was. That's the way it made me feel. The counselor they sent me up was totally useless. She was afraid of me. I yelled at her. But then again I was hurting very much at that time. If she can't handle it, she shouldn't have been in there trying to handle it. Well I didn't yell at her. I yelled to her about what happened and how I felt. Here I was waiting for break and now I'm in the hospital, totally helpless, because of some other fool's stupidity. The real problem with the whole thing is it wasn't my fault. I had nothing to do with it. I had absolutely no control over it. That's what scares me the most is I really don't have any control.

I'm fine when I'm in control. When someone else is in control I get really... whatever you want to call it.

It's not like this is the first time you've been hurt... You've had a fair amount of bumps and bruises...

Of course, bike accidents, car accidents.

What makes this different?

Having control of it. (He goes on to explain that the bike and car accidents are "his fault"...)

(transition)

What happened when you got out of the hospital?

Mainly, uh, I really didn't start having nightmares until quite awhile later. There was so much pain in the hospital it kept me from thinking. It's kind of hard to explain. There was such so much physical pain in the hospital that my mind was focused on that I guess you'd say. It really didn't faze me until after maybe a month or so when I was home, maybe a few months. Time is a blur.

Then I started having serious nightmares about burning. People would scare the piss out of me if they lit a cigarette. I couldn't light the stove. The smell of gas would scare the ever living piss out of me. It made me feel so weak and helpless. It was just so safe to sit on the couch and stay there...and I did.

You didn't notice this reaction when you first got home . . . there was a delay to it?

I went fishing the day I got home... hands were all bandaged up, could hardly hold it. I thought everything was going to be... you know... no problem. Then...it seems like the more physically better I got the more mentally handicapped I got at the same time. Everything didn't just pop up and all of a sudden I was a raving maniac. Ascared of his own shadow. I didn't even realize it, because maybe after the explosion I was sheltered from all of those things without even knowing it. As I got healthier and back into the real world, those things were there. I don't know...that's the best way that I can explain it.

(transition)

What were some of the first things that you noticed... concerns, worries, fears.

Well, first it was just a fear of everything. Anything that was powered. That even had the slightest chance of burning or exploding... the car, things like that. Any kind of mechanical thing, I couldn't get near them. I'm still having a hard time standing directly next to something that is running. And it irritates me.

Electricity or something running on gas?

Mostly gas, but electricity, at first really did bother me, too. I just kept picturing in my mind the thing blowing up and throwing shrapnel all over the place, or something like that. I could actually picture it ripping through my skin. It scared me to the point where I kept getting hollower and hollower and hollower, and shrunk on to the couch.

You became a pretty good example of a couch potato there for a while.

Yah, I could write the book.

It was safe being in your home. . . I don't want to put the words in your mouth. . .

No, no cause those are the words that I've always used all along. My couch was very safe; I felt very safe on my couch. I was in control on my couch. You know, as long as I sat on it and didn't get up and leave. Like most people who don't *have a life... I did a lot of sleeping, which is very "unpar for the course" considering I lived on six hours of sleep a night.*

These feelings that you all of a sudden got in touch with, to coin a phrase, were pretty new...

They were all new. Everybody can deal with pain. Its fear that I am having a hard time dealing with. Cause I never really... I mean everyone has been afraid...but I've never been afraid to deal with it. Why am I so afraid to deal with this?

That is a good question. I'm not sure I have a good answer except to say that your reaction is normal considering what you've been through. Tell me about the nightmares.

Yeah, I noticed that a lot. I really started to have nightmares constantly. Weird things, too. I'll tell you what. Mostly, really strange dreams. As far as explaining some of them, I don't know. But they'd make me wake up sweating. The main dream I had constantly was that guy on the ambulance. He really messed me up a lot. He kept coming back and back and back, asking me over and over what happened: "Am I alright?" What was I going to tell the guy: "You got no lips, pal. You're gonna die."

You knew that when you looked at him in the ambulance?

God, he's lucky he did. It was horrible.

(transition)

What didn't people understand?

What really irritated me most about... the whole situation was everybody said: "You look good. Got lucky." Let me fill your sneakers with gasoline... see how lucky you feel.

That's what they would say to you: "You got lucky"?

Yuh, pretty lucky. Look good. Could of been worse. Gee, I'm sorry it wasn't. Does this mean I'm good now. All betterer...What do you think, am I betterer?

I play this videotape at most of my workshops because the words, the tone, the feelings of this individual capture the experience of PTSD in a way that textbooks or lectures are limited.

Individuals suffering from Post-traumatic Stress Disorder should be referred for ongoing psychotherapy with a professional who has received training and has experience working with victims of trauma.

SUMMARY

The Essence of Psychological Trauma Is the Loss of Faith That There Is Order and Continuity in Life.

Trauma Occurs When One Loses the Sense of Having a Safe Place to Retreat Within or Outside Oneself to Deal with Frightening Emotions or Experiences.

This Results in a State of Helplessness, a Feeling that One's Actions Have No Bearing on the Outcome of One's Life.

Bessel van der Kolk, 1987

Chapter 5

DYNAMICS AND DEFINITIONS INVOLVED WITH DIFFERENT TYPES OF CRISES

At this point we are looking at the critical incident beyond the specific scope of the ESP. In the next section of this manual we will be transitioning to examine the incident from the perspective of the victim. It is important to remember that as we talk about the victim, the same issues, dynamics and factors also resonate with the ESP who may develop PTSD as a result of unresolved CIS.

When intervening with victims, or conducting debriefings for the ESP, one needs to be concerned with the specific crisis to make sure that all situational variables that define a critical incident are considered. In this chapter, the important factors of which to be aware when doing any kind of intervention are discussed. By the end of the intervention, be it a formal debriefing or an individual assessment, the people conducting the debriefing should have a good understanding of these variables. The expectation is not that each one of these variables is "covered" during a debriefing; rather, they are factors to be referenced and mentioned during the education phase of a debriefing. (See Chapter 9, Guidelines for Conducting Debriefings.)

SITUATIONAL FACTORS AFFECTING EXTENT OF STRESS

The following is an elaboration on the work by Demi and Miles (1983), from the article "Understanding Physiologic Reactions to Disaster." Once again, be sure to keep in mind that these variables apply to individuals (victims), communities, or workplace settings.

Warning

A warning is **information**; the less warning, the more profound the emotional impact. As an example, an earthquake allows for little to no warning, and therefore, people are caught unprepared and feel vulnerable and out of control. A hurricane may be just as devastating, but usually the people have some time in which to take steps to prepare themselves both physically and emotionally.

Nature of the Crisis

Often the type of emotional response is different to a man-made situation (criminal act, negligence, etc.) versus an *act of God*. In general, people feel more rage, responsibility, guilt, when it is "man-made". In those situations, the sense perhaps is that something might have been done to avoid the incident. Often victims of crime go through reactions of self-blame and guilt around not preventing the incident. Common statements are heard such as, "I should have noticed the person following me..." or "We should have installed an alarm system." The feelings of blame and responsibility may be directed toward others: "If the legal system were better..." or "The equipment is so faulty, it was just a matter of time before someone got hurt."

When a trauma is considered to be *natural* or an *act of God*, the feeling is that this is a terrible thing to have happened, but no direct responsibility can be assigned and it could not have been prevented. The self-directed guilt or other directed rage associated with responsibility is diminished. Those intense feelings of frustration may have no place to go or to be directed except as anger at God or perhaps as a loss of religious faith.

It Is Important to Acknowledge the Feelings and Not to Try to Talk the Individual Out of His/Her Feelings.

Severity of the Crisis

Clearly a positive correlation exists between the severity of the crisis and the reactions of people involved, be they victims, observers, or ESPs. One must question, how do we define severity? By the number of casualties? By the degree of trauma to one individual? By the age and perspective of the victim? A child would react very differently to a minor head wound that is bleeding profusely than would an adult. A police officer would react differently to finding a person who has attempted suicide by cutting his/her wrist than would a family member. As was discussed in the first section on general stress, an essential point to remember is that the incident or the objective facts of the trauma are not necessarily the most important, but rather different persons' perceptions and/or associations to the event are.

Physical Proximity

The closer one lives to an incident and the victims, the stronger the stress reaction. Living in the town in which a fire, accident, or earthquake has occurred is much more stressful than if it occurs in another community. Oftentimes, in small communities, many of the ESP must respond to a situation in which they are dealing with people whom they know. They may have gone to school with the victim, dated his/her cousin, grew up down the street, or may even be a relative. ESPs report that knowing the victim makes the performance of their duties a more emotionally difficult task.

In the case of a large disaster, if the ESP must be concerned for his/her own welfare, or is worrying about his/her family, this generates **role conflict**. It is only natural to feel distracted from the performance of duties if the ESP is worried about someone in his/her family being injured in the same major disaster. It distracts from the individual's ability to focus their attention on the person(s) and task(s) at hand.

PERSONAL FACTORS AFFECTING INDIVIDUALS' RESPONSES

Personal factors describe characteristics that may influence how the individual responds to a critical incident. As part of the intervention, the professional needs to be sure that the following factors have been addressed.

Psychological Proximity

At the risk of stating the obvious, the more an individual is impacted personally by an incident, the greater the risk is of not coping with the event. This applies to the victim, witness, or ESP. In a similar fashion as the **physical proximity**, if a crisis hits close to home on an emotional level, it may exacerbate the stress response. As an example, if an ESP is intervening with a child victim and he/she has a child of a similar age, the tendency is to have an automatic identification process.

I provide an EAP to a client-company in which a woman developed breast cancer. She worked in a small, close-knit department staffed predominantly by women. The effect of this woman's illness had varied impacts on the women in that department. All of them expressed concern over a serious illness to a close friend. Many were concerned over their own health and the possibility of developing the disease. Several had lost family members as a result of the same disease and this woman's illness rekindled a grief reaction. These are all examples of psychological proximity.

Coping Skills

The rule of thumb is that those who have had problems coping with negative events in the past may be more prone to experiencing difficulty with a present crisis. People tend to utilize the same defense mechanisms when dealing with stress. If stressful events have been handled poorly in the past, the likelihood is greater that the individual may mismanage another difficult situation. This is especially true if the most recent event is in any way similar to or associated with a previous situation.

Concurrent Stressors

Stress is cumulative; if there are many other losses, changes, or transitions in an individual's life, another crisis (especially dealing with trauma) may be the "last straw." An example may be the individual who has gone through a divorce as well as the death of a parent in the past year. He/she is more vulnerable to the impact of job-related stress than someone who's life has been more stable.

From a different perspective, Gail Lenehan (December, 1986) reported in her article, "Emotional Impact of Trauma," that "those experiencing stress may be more likely to sustain trauma." Further, she cited other studies indicating that "psychological stress was found in 40% of one sample of trauma patients." Again, in another sample, "28% of drivers causing fatal accidents had experienced some emotionally disturbing event less than 6 months before their crashes."

The literature abounds with references to the correlation between stress and vulnerability. People under stress tend to be more prone to accidents, illnesses, and other crises, and their capacity to resolve the stress is diminished. It may become a vicious cycle: stress leads to a diminished capacity, which may result in more stressful events, which further diminish one's capacity to cope.

Role Conflict/Overload

If a person is in the position of being the victim or patient, but professionally is an ESP or in the helping professions, this may place him/her in a difficult emotional bind. An example of this was told to me by a nurse who was admitted to the hospital for surgery. During her first day post-surgery she was in her room with the curtain pulled, restricted to her bed in a weakened condition. The patient in the other bed in the room suddenly "threw a clot." Major chaos ensued, with the code blue team descending upon the room. No one was aware that the RN patient was in the room until after they had pronounced the other woman dead. The RN heard the entire procedure, including comments and swearing when the defibrillation machine was not working properly. Upon finding her in the room, the hospital staff was very responsive, but she reported being totally intellectualized and clinical until she was ambulatory and no longer feeling confined/restricted/helpless. Then she had a major outburst of feelings including tears, fears, guilt, and rage that she could not respond to help the lady. She also was enraged at the hospital for their seeming incompetence. None of these feelings surfaced until she was feeling back in control of her body and able to function.

Previous Experience

Those with little experience or training may be at a higher risk. The greater the amount of experience with trauma, the greater the ability to cope. However, a certain point may be reached at which the accumulated experience may develop into a case of burnout if it has not been resolved properly. To draw the line on this factor is difficult. A department that has little trauma activity may be effected greatly by a single car accident with a single fatality. Similarly, a metropolitan department that responds to a lot of calls may have much experience, but also a great many members with various stages of burnout.

Age

Age also plays a factor in coping with crisis and trauma. Stated simply, the younger the ESP, the greater the tendency to experience a stronger stress reaction. Research comparing the effects of warfare on the Vietnam veteran to the WWII vet indicated that the average age of the Vietnam vet was 19 as compared to 26 for the WWII soldier. Certainly the two war experiences were quite different; however, some believe that this is part of the explanation for the Vietnam veterans' more difficult adjustment after their war experience. It seems that younger adults may have a stronger reaction to trauma than someone who is just a few years their senior.

Temporal Proximity

During one of my recent workshops, a participant described a situation in which a tragedy occurred during a happy festive occasion. A discussion ensued as others reported knowledge of similar incidents where a tragedy occurred in close temporal proximity to a significant event/holiday. Thus, the two events, one tragic and sad and the other festive and happy, become joined paradoxically together forever. Examples of this might be a (1) death of a family member close to (or at) a wedding, (2) traumatic car accident on or near a holiday/birthday/anniversary, or (3) diagnosis of a life threatening illness coinciding with the announcement of a pregnancy in the family. As we discussed this juxtaposition, it became obvious that individuals experiencing this type of *temporal proximity* would be very vulnerable, as it combines *psychological proximity, concurrent stressors* and *role conflict.*

TRAUMA RECOVERY PHASES

Research reported by Frederick (1987) indicated that trauma recovery has three phases. Although these phases apply to the victim, we must remember that the same phases are applicable to an ESP, a community, or a work environment.

Phase 1: Pre-impact Phase

Phase 1, the pre-impact phase, is the time when the individual is aware that a crisis is about to develop. For the victim, it may be a matter of seconds, a moment of warning—time to prepare as the *fight or flight response* is activated. For the ESP, this refers to the *information* and *warning* factors as described at the beginning of this chapter. It is an initial effort to prepare for what may be experienced.

Phase 2: Impact Phase

Phase 2, the impact phase, is the experiencing of the actual event. During this phase, survival efforts are initiated. ESPs often describe feeling as if they are operating in a state of *autopilot*; they perform their functions with a sense of detachment and emotional disconnection. Some ESPs (and victims) report that they experience the situation as if they are outside of themselves, impassively watching. The victim may describe being in a state of shock, depersonalization, or derealization. These are psychiatric symptoms describing dissociative conditions in which the individual experiences himself/herself as functioning in a "dream-like" state similar to having a déjà vu experience, but for long periods of time. Or, the person may feel like the world around him/her has a sense of unreality similar to the type of reality distortion that one may experience with certain drugs.

Phase 3: Post Impact Phase

Phase 3, the post impact phase, begins shortly after the event and may last at least two years. Frederick further divided this phase into three subphases: *honeymoon, disillusionment, reconstruction.*

Honeymoon. The honeymoon subphase is a brief period (hours to weeks) during which the survivor/victim experiences a sense of relief at having survived (whether it be a disfiguring surgery, a violent crime, an accident, an earthquake).

Disillusionment. During the disillusionment subphase the survivor realizes that a permanent disruption and sense of loss has occurred as a result of the crisis. The person may feel anger, resentment, frustration, etc. This is often manifested through contradictory blaming of others while concurrently looking to others to fix the problems. The focus of this blame may be directed at physicians, the government, the legal system, the spouse, God, or any other source. This may be a time of significant turmoil and change. Often people feel the need to make dramatic changes in their lives; some leave spouses, jobs, and/or geographical location by moving to other parts of the country. During this phase, people may become depressed and have difficulty coping. Often this appears to be a delayed reaction to the trauma and may not be understood by others close to the person. Education for the victim as well as the family prior to this stage is essential.

Reconstruction. During this subphase, the victim/survivor takes responsibility for rebuilding his/her physical and/or emotional life. It is often a slow and arduous process that requires much support and understanding from others.

Summary of Trauma Recovery Phases

These phases and subphases may apply to the individual and/or communities (including work settings) in which a trauma has occurred. For the individual, the phase could be as a result of an accident, a violent crime, or surgery. A community or workplace may experience these phases as a result of a major disaster. Recognize and remember that the course through these phases does not necessarily go in an orderly progression. An individual may jump from **honeymoon** to **reconstruction**, then go back to **disillusionment**, then again to **reconstruction,** and once more to **honeymoon**. As mentioned, during **disillusionment** the individual will become very involved actively in making significant changes in his/her life. Initially, he/she may experience a return to the **honeymoon** phase, hoping that the change will help him/her to feel better. As reality sets in, he/she may find that the change did not help and that he/she may reexperience stronger feelings of **disillusionment**.

STAGES IN DYING AND DEATH EXPERIENCE

During the 1970s, psychiatrist Elisabeth Kubler-Ross became very well-known for her work in the area of death and dying. Since then, her ideas have been generalized to include other areas of loss. Whether it be a body part as a result of surgery, a loved one as a result of death, self-esteem and security as a result of victimization, or home and personal belongings from a disaster, Kubler-Ross'(1970) work on death and dying is extremely relevant. She postulated that as part of the dying and death experience, an individual goes through stages.

Denial Stage

An initial reflexive reaction often experienced is one of denial that protects one from emotional pain. The person may be in a state of shock and actually not be aware of what is being said to them or what is happening to them. People receiving a serious diagnosis may go from one doctor to another not believing what is being told to them.

Bargaining Stage

As part of the acceptance process, the wall of denial begins to develop some breaks; bargaining begins. The individual begins to understand that something serious is happening to him/her, but he/she will still attempt to control it by *making deals*. An example of this is the man who was told that he had cancer and bargained that he would give up drinking, go to church, and give money to charity if God would let him live.

Anger Stage

As the individual realizes that he/she does not have control over the process and experiences the intrusion and the disruption in his/her life, he/she may feel scared and angry. As the disease progresses and impacts on abilities and competence, the person may bounce from feelings of anger to bouts of depression.

Depression Stage

The depression stage is different than being sad or low. This is a deeper sense of despair and desperation. Often the individual loses sight of any positive aspects of life, and any sense of hope or future is diminished.

Acceptance Stage

During the acceptance stage, individuals are *letting go*, accepting that their life is going to be shortened. For some, this is a time when they can find peace and a deep inner sense of strength. For others, it is a resignation with depressive overtones.

I participated in several of Dr. Kubler-Ross' workshops in which she described that these stages are, in fact, not stages but rather sets of feelings through which an individual may cycle. It is clear that Kubler-Ross' stages seem to describe a similar process to those described by Frederick.

NORMALITY OF TRAUMA REACTION

Whether the trauma is the result of an accident, a violent crime or even a surgical intervention, people experiencing trauma often seem to experience a disturbance in the expression and regulation of emotions. Often, the disturbance manifests itself as a blunting of affect (feeling) and a seeming shallowness or absence of emotionality. Remember that this is often the natural reaction to the first stages of response to trauma. The "ego constriction" may be a necessary conservation of emotional energy. Or perhaps, the person is worried about losing total control if he/she gives access to any emotion. It is essential that this defense be allowed and that intervening personnel not attempt to *help* the person *get in touch with their true feelings*. *True feelings* will emerge as the person feels capable of dealing with them; often this may be several weeks or months after the event. In a medical setting, trauma patients should be considered normal, and psychiatric labeling should be avoided.

Victims of trauma often feel that they have lost their identity, and they grieve the loss of themselves. Several patients with whom I have worked have asked: "Will I ever feel like my old self?" When faced with this type of quandary, remember to avoid false reassurances. The essential point is to help individuals understand that they will not always feel as confused and out of control of their feelings and their lives. Further, through the (painful) healing process, the goal is to develop a new sense of self. On more than one occasion I have found myself saying, "You cannot go back to whom you were. The experience that you have been through will leave some scars. However, you can go forward and perhaps become a stronger, more secure and more sensitive person."

Family members also need assistance in coming to terms with the "loss" of the person. As was so poignantly described in Case 3 in Chapter 4, Post-traumatic Stress Disorder, once the victim has physically healed, be it from assault, surgery, or another form of victimization, often the expectation is that "everything will be o.k...." Often, only after the physical healing has been completed can the true emotional healing begin. Family members need assistance in coping with their own feelings of loss and frustration around the incident. A traumatic incident to one's partner is a very difficult experience for the *significant other* of the victim. Marriages may undergo a great amount of tension, and the victim and partner should be made aware of this potential stress. Follow-up consultation is highly recommended.

"AN ABNORMAL REACTION TO AN ABNORMAL SITUATION IS NORMAL BEHAVIOR."

Viktor Frankl (1966)

Chapter **6**

CRITICAL INCIDENT STRESS RESPONSE (CISR):STRATEGIES AND INTERVENTIONS TO DEAL WITH CIS

The Emergency Service Professional (ESP) can in no way avoid situations that may result in Critical Incident Stress (CIS). The only thing that can be done is for each individual/department to be aware of the impact and to make efforts to counter the negative effects of CIS by developing *Critical Incident Stress Response (CISR)* programs. To that end, the following are suggestions to be incorporated as part of a CISR program to help ameliorate the effects of intervening with trauma and crises.

POLICIES, PROCEDURES, PROGRAMS
(The Three Ps)

For the Department/Agency on an Ongoing Basis

1. CIS education should be included as part of a basic orientation and training for new employees. Every

emergency services department (police, fire, hospital, crisis) should mandate that each employee receive a minimum of three hours of education/training on CIS.

2. Ongoing CIS training should be provided for peer counselors, supervisory staff, and ranking officers. For these categories of personnel, an all-day training seminar should be available in conjunction with ongoing discussion/supervision with a mental health professional.

3. A committee should be developed that will formulate agency-wide policies and procedures regarding CIS education, training, and response.

Each emergency service organization, hospital, high risk profession, and Employee Assistance Program (EAP) should have a protocol that describes the "three Ps" for Critical Incident Stress Response (CISR). It should cover, as a minimum, the following components (these are not listed in any specific order):

a. Define what constitutes a Critical Incident within the context of the specific organization.

b. If there is a Critical Incident, formulate policy for length of time at the scene and time off after the CI (if necessary).

c. Clarify how CISR is to be utilized within the organization and for what benefit/purpose.

d. Delineate the chain of command describing who is responsible for initiating a CISR and who shall conduct the debriefing(s).

e. Develop a statement regarding confidentiality with respect to any formal debriefings. Specific concern with respect to investigations must be addressed.

f. Develop guidelines for mandatory versus voluntary participation in debriefings, and "on-the-clock" or other payment status.

g. Outline clear directives limiting communication with media and designation of media liaison.

h. Identify who conducts the debriefings. Will it be peer counselors from the department/organization, mental health agency, or the Employee Assistance Program?

i. If the agency/department is going to utilize peer counselors, describe the level of training and any professional backup support required.

j. In the case of serious injury or death of an employee or a large scale disaster, describe support services available for family members.

k. Designate an individual as the CISR coordinator. This individual is responsible for implementing and organizing the aforementioned **policies, procedures, and programs.**

Many departments/agencies get caught up in all of the policy and procedures, and do not feel that they can move ahead and conduct any debriefings until they have dotted all of the i's and crossed all of the t's. Many times the policy and procedures will evolve as an agency/department begins to respond to Critical Incidents. Policies and procedures must be reviewed on an ongoing basis. This should include a process by which the entire department is surveyed regarding their experiences with CIS training, debriefings, etc. The purpose of such a review process is to allow the staff to feel included in the development of the program and to facilitate further discussion of CIS experiences among the staff.

If the Critical Incident Stress/Trauma (CIS/T) team is coordinating the interventions for a large organization or geographic area, careful attention must be paid to implementing a clear and concise chain of command. In my consultations to hospitals that are setting up teams, often "turf" issues exist among the different departments and/or disciplines. These issues need to be worked out prior to instituting any formal program. One method that has been suggested is that the CIS/T coordinator position and other organizational roles be rotated on a yearly basis. By doing so, different departments or disciplines will feel involved and that they have a significant role.

As Ongoing Strategies for the Individual ESP

1. Maintain a good social network; friends and activities can help to distract from the stress of the job.

2. Participate in an exercise program that promotes cardiovascular fitness.

3. Maintain a good diet that limits fats, salts, and cholesterol.

4. Limit the amount of alcohol and other controlled substances.

At the Time of a Critical Incident

1. The supervisory staff should be aware of the emotional state of its personnel. As part of the supervisory staff's training, they should gain an understanding of CIS and know the signs and symptoms. They should know how to address the issue with the people with whom they work.

2. In long duration/high intensity situations, personnel should be rotated from high intensity to low exposure. Short "defusing" interventions should be attempted to assess the emotional status of the personnel. Certainly this is not always possible, but it should be considered whenever conceivable.

3. At the time of an incident, a brief "defusing" is often considered to be helpful. This may take the form of a momentary acknowledgement by others that the incident is extraordinary. Some individuals need to take a minute or two to talk very briefly about what is happening around them. These actions are not debriefings (which take place after an event); rather they are momentary "time-outs" in order to reenergize and return to the task at hand.

4. After an incident, time should be taken to debrief at least informally about the experience. Often this takes place in small groups; however, a formal debriefing is thought to acknowledge the experience and the feelings.

If an Individual Is Experiencing Symptoms of CIS

1. Have the person attempt to eat regularly even though a disturbance of appetite may be experienced; healthy, light foods are suggested.

2. Help him/her recognize that sleep may be disrupted after a CI. The individual should not toss and turn in bed attempting to will himself/herself to sleep. He/she should feel free to get up, read, watch TV, write about the experience, or talk to someone. Sleep will come as the person rids himself/herself of the *emotional toxins*. People should be reassured that disturbed sleep is often a symptom of a CIS reaction.

3. Help the individual to realize that the feelings, thoughts, and visions will diminish over time and that the use of alcohol or drugs will compound rather than relieve the problem.

4. Help the person to talk by enabling him/her to utilize peer support, EAP, clergy, spouses, and/or friends.

5. Encourage the person to remain active and maintain a regular schedule of activities.

Remember that CIS Is the Body and Mind's Coping Response of a Normal Person to an Abnormal Situation. If Feelings Are Shared, Understood, and Accepted by One's Self and Others, the Recovery from CIS Will Be More Rapid and More Thorough.

Chapter **7**

REACTIONS
OF OTHERS

Over time, the ESP develops a variety of defense mechanisms to cope with the stress of working with crisis and trauma as a regular part of the job. As was discussed earlier in this manual, one of the more common mechanisms is the unconscious transition into ***autopilot***. Certainly this is a beneficial protective defense against the anguish of seeing other humans in pain, turmoil, or the victims of traumatic injury. However, for many ESPs the autopilot response is easy to initiate as it becomes conditioned in response to the sound of an alarm, a radio call, the ER doors opening, etc. Many ESPs describe that, as automatically as the autopilot response is activated, it is difficult to terminate the response. Many may return home after their shift and still be in autopilot mode. The family members may experience the individual as being distant, remote and uncaring. The autopilot response tends to be all-inclusive. The result is as if a protective shield descends and mutes all incoming and outgoing emotional interactions including loving feelings and feelings of intimacy. In fact, people who have experienced both CIS and PTSD have reported that they may experience strong emotional reactions about the event at times of relaxation or intimacy (sexual or otherwise). These are times when one allows his/her defenses to relax. As the defenses come down, the CIS/PTSD symptoms may develop.

OPENNESS VERSUS CLOSURE WITH FAMILY MEMBERS

Family members may sense the distance or discomfort and not understand what it is all about. Oftentimes they will personalize the remoteness, assuming that it is a reflection of something about the relationship. If family members attempt to inquire, the ESP may not be open to discussing his/her feelings for several reasons: (1) he/she does not want to appear vulnerable, (2) he/she wishes to protect the family from what they have witnessed/experienced, or (3) he/she is unable to respond at that time because he/she is experiencing CIS.

SPOUSE/SIGNIFICANT OTHER BECOMES THE VICTIM

Remember that families of ESPs may experience a mini-CIS crisis of their own in response to seeing their loved ones overwhelmed by emotional feelings as a result of CIS. Now their husband/wife (the ESP) is in the position of the victim and family members are attempting to be the intervening personnel.

DEBRIEFING STAFF AND THEIR FAMILIES

In situations in which an entire shift or department is impacted by a critical incident, information should be made available to the families of the ESP regarding what has transpired. In situations in which an ESP has been injured or killed in the performance of his/her duty, it is considered *imperative* to have a debriefing for the families as well as the personnel. These should be held as two separate meetings since the ESP may feel stifled discussing their reactions with non-ESPs. In a similar way, spouses may feel a sense of camaraderie with each other and might feel uncomfortable discussing their concerns with their ESP spouses in the meeting.

ESP WORK AND POTENTIAL EFFECT ON THE FAMILY

Working in an *at risk* profession is certainly difficult for the professional. However, those who love and care about him/her also may be in a stressful situation. Further, if the studies from HEW indicating a higher than average divorce rate for police officers represent a trend, then the evidence is available to suggest that employment in the emergency services may be difficult on a marriage. This is a complicated issue. It is not known if these professions attract individuals who are not *adept* at marriage, or, if there is something about the work and the defenses required that interferes with interpersonal relationships. Regardless, stress at home may serve only to cultivate the development of **burnout** and, hence, interfere with the performance of duties and responsibilities.

TIME PLUS PROFESSIONAL ASSISTANCE NEEDED

With respect to the families of victims of crisis and/or trauma, much of the aforementioned discussion is relevant. However, being the victim of a serious crisis or trauma may have serious symptoms that do not resolve for quite a period of time. People involved in crises or those who have been traumatically victimized often report a disruption in their interpersonal relationships. As was discussed previously in Chapters 4 and 5, the victim of a serious crisis or trauma may not develop difficulties immediately, and it may take up to two years to feel that a certain level of normalcy has been reestablished. People not receiving some form of psychotherapy often attempt to cope with the emotional disruption through a variety of methods that may be self-destructive. Often shame and anger are involved, which may get focused on and played out in a significant relationship.

My strong recommendation is that victims receive ongoing psychotherapy to assist in their recovery. Further, their "significant other" should be included in the therapeutic process.

Certainly this does not mean to imply that he/she be at each session, but that the couple also must be viewed as "the victim" if it is to survive intact.

When planning interventions around crisis/trauma, the recommendation is that the team look at three levels of involved individuals. Having done so the decision may be to intervene only with one of these groups; however during the strategizing phase, efforts should be made to consider responses to three distinct groups of involved persons.

Primary Level

These are individuals who have been affected directly by the incident and/or witnessed directly the traumatic event. These people may be in need of medical attention and not immediately available for or receptive to psychological interventions. These people may experience the most significant reactions, which may be delayed until after medical treatment has been discontinued.

In the case of CIS with ESPs, the primary level would involve those professionals responding to the situation. There may be different degrees of intensity depending upon whether the ESP was "first on the scene" or responded as a "backup" team.

Secondary Level

These are family members and significant others of people in the primary group. Often, they will need supportive intervention, but unless careful consideration is given, they may be forgotten while most of the focus is directed toward the primary victims.

Tertiary Level

These are individuals who are considered in **consonance** to the people in the primary level. The term "consonance" means related to, in harmony with, but in a more meaningful sense. Perhaps an example may help to clarify the significance of the term. It is known that if you have two pianos in a room and you play a key on one of them, the corresponding strings of the other piano will vibrate. In the same way, people experience a sense of consonance during times of crisis. If a fire fighter is injured, other fire fighters experience consonance. If a bank is robbed, other bank tellers in other branches may experience a feeling of anxiety and vulnerability. If a woman is assaulted in the parking lot of her place of employment, all other women in that workplace may experience a corresponding sense of emotional "vibration"... consonance. When we respond to crisis and trauma, we need to remember the third level of individuals who may be affected by the incident. These are not primary victims or their significant others, but rather people in the workplace in consonant roles.

Another group of people in this category would be individuals who had a significant work/personal relationship with the primary victims. Often, they are expected to respond in a supportive way or to return to work as if they had been unaffected. These people, too, may benefit from some type of intervention.

It is not expected that there always will be the need for an intervention at all of these levels. However, when thinking through and planning an appropriate response, think beyond the primary level.

TRAUMA AND CRISIS IN THE WORKPLACE

The Centers for Disease Control estimate that approximately 10 million work-related injuries and 7,000 work-related deaths occur each year. I am probably "preaching to the choir" when I say that the manner in which a crisis/trauma in the workplace is handled is extremely important to the resolution of trauma for individual employees. Further, a workplace crisis/trauma may have far-reaching impact on all employees and subsequently the organization as a whole.

EXAMPLES OF CRISES AND/OR TRAUMA SITUATIONS

As indicated in the previous section of this manual, discussing the workplace is not a simple matter; a variety of situations and a multitude of variables are involved. Interventions as a mental health professional, human resource personnel, or EAP personnel must be customized to the specific situation. The following are examples of some of the types of situations that are considered crises and/or trauma in the workplace:

1. One individual is hurt as a result of his/her own negligence.

2. An individual is injured as a result of the negligence of another employee.

3. Many people are injured as a result of a large accident.

4. Someone dies suddenly outside of work.

5. Someone is mugged/robbed/raped in a parking lot by a non-employee.

6. An employee is assaulted by another employee.

7. A teacher is assaulted by a student.

8. A teacher is accused of inappropriate behavior by a student.

9. An employee is arrested for drug dealing at or outside of work.

10. An employee is diagnosed as having a serious illness requiring hospitalization.

11. A convenience store, bank, department store, or delivery truck is robbed.

12. A major layoff of personnel (euphemistically referred to as "downsizing," "trimming the fat") occurs.

TRAUMA IN THE WORKPLACE

The list of 12 represents a sampling of the types of situations that may be considered traumatic and/or critical in a workplace environment.

Once again, it is essential to refer to the **situational** and **personal factors** as described previously in Chapter 5 as they apply to critical incidents in the workplace as well.

At this point, we need to review the differentiation between Critical Incident Stress and crisis\trauma. CIS is a term reserved for what Emergency Service Professionals (ESPs) experience. A significant difference between critical incidents for ESPs and crisis/trauma in the workplace is that ESPs are trained and prepared to confront these situations as part of their professional experience. Trauma in the workplace usually is unexpected and not considered to be a part of the "job description."

At the time of a crisis, it is imperative to respond to the people in the workplace as one would respond to a family in crisis. Many workers spend more time with people at work than they do with their own family members. Some of the most important relationships develop through the work environment. We work with, eat with, and socialize with people at work. We share holidays, births, deaths, graduations, and marriages with people at work.

During a crisis in the workplace, information regarding the incident is of vital importance. The concern over privacy for the individual(s) involved must be respected; however, the rest of the "workplace family" should be provided with as much information as possible. This is done in an effort to limit the impact of the *rumor mill,* which tends to grind very rapidly at times of crisis. If people do not have information, they tend to create it out of "bits n' pieces," fantasy, distortion, and fear. This is a natural tendency for people in crisis; however, it should be dissuaded. There must be an ongoing process through which the provision of accurate up-to-date information can be made available to people. Do not forget those employees who have been on vacation during the time of the incident. They may return to *old news* and be in a different stage of reaction than the rest of their fellow employees. One person needs to be designated as **information coordinator,** and an easy method needs to be established for people to have access to this individual. By having one person as the *info-gatekeeper,* everyone will be guaranteed of hearing the same story, and protect others who do not know what to tell people.

As a result of a crisis in the workplace, the work force (or portions of it) may go through the same reactions/stages/phases as described in Chapter 5 for a victim of trauma. People may experience an immediate sense of relief or grief. However, there are often additional responses as the workplace goes into a post impact stage. In the case of an accident in the workplace, the most notable reactions of others is initially grief followed by guilt, anger, and fear. This tends to be true particularly if there is any suggestion of negligence or safety violations.

Similar to our homes, most people expect that the workplace is a safe place. As in the case of an accident/crime/death/victimization/crisis on a personal level, a crisis in the workplace may tend to bring out all of the underlying tensions, problems, and difficulties that lay dormant below the surface. An unexpected crisis/trauma leaves people feeling **threatened, abandoned, vulnerable, unprotected, and betrayed.** The natural response to these feelings is often anger and/or depression.

At the time of a trauma or crisis in the workplace, a need exists for

1. information;

2. increased visibility on the part of management;

3. formal and informal debriefings;

4. time off for funeral, legal proceedings, and medical treatment; and,

5. in the case of an accident resulting in a death, a formal acknowledgement
(newspaper notice, donation, scholarship fund, or plaque on a conference room door).

Layoffs, Downsizing, and Other Transition Crises

During the 1990s, many corporate transitions have resulted in *layoffs, cutbacks, and downsizing*. We must remember that these are part of the corporate nomenclature and sound neutral and impersonal but have very significant implications for these individuals involved. My definition of a layoff or downsizing is as follows:

To take away someone's livelihood such that his/her life-style is at least severely threatened if not permanently disrupted. This often occurs at a time of life when the individual has one or more major financial commitments.

To understand the impact of a layoff in the workplace, it may be helpful to use the metaphor of a patient requiring surgery: An individual develops symptoms that indicate a need for an evaluation. A problem is defined, and a tentative diagnosis is made requiring that some interventions be initiated. As a variety of treatments are introduced, it is discovered that the illness/disease remains, and further, more extensive procedures become necessary and surgery is scheduled. The surgeon may perform a highly technical piece of work, removing some life-threatening tumor or repairing a ruptured organ. However, as we all know, after a surgery, the patient is very vulnerable and requires close care and a wide variety of ancillary services. Many times a surgery may be successful, but the patient dies as a result of infection or unforeseen complications. Further, as any one knows who has had surgery, although we may be diagnosed as "ill" when we enter the hospital, we usually feel worse upon discharge and for some time thereafter.

The same dynamics apply when a corporate system is ill or malfunctioning. Within a corporate system, a layoff or downsizing is no different from surgical amputation or resection. In order for the whole body to survive, a traumatic event must take place. A decision is made and a portion of the corporate body is removed. In surgery, a procedure on one organ of the body impacts upon and involves the entire physiological system. This is true for a corporate system as well. If 20% of the sales force is to be laid off, this affects manufacturing, service, Research and Development, etc. If we are replacing blood vessels in the heart with veins from the leg, both areas of surgery require close monitoring and interventions. If we are transplanting an organ from another "foreign" system, efforts must be made to control for rejection. The same is true for departmental or corporate mergers.

As difficult as surgery (or a layoff) may be, the healing and recovery is often a longer and more difficult process. And, if not done with adequate skill and available resources, the corporate patient also may succumb to complications and infections as represented by the following:

**RESENTMENT TOWARD MANAGEMENT
ISOLATION FROM COWORKERS
INCREASE IN ABSENTEEISM
DECREASE IN WORK PRODUCTIVITY
INCREASE IN ACCIDENTS
INCREASE IN WORKMAN'S COMPENSATION CASES
INCREASED TURNOVER IN WORK FORCE**

Large companies going through personnel transitions must realize that after the downsizing, much emotional healing must be done. In an effort to save money, people are laid off; however, this may cost the company a great deal extra if the process is not handled appropriately.

Recent studies indicate that some individuals may take being laid off as seriously as the death of a family member. Especially hard-hit are the "breadwinners" and people who have worked for many years. For many people, one's career is a large part of one's identity. Losing a job is more than losing a paycheck.

For the survivors, yet another situation occurs. Often they have *survivor guilt*; how come I survived and my coworker was laid off? Resentment occurs from things such as job responsibilities may be different and/or departments may have changed. They may have lost friends and colleagues or be receiving less salary or benefits as a result of the transition. I caution managers not to expect that the survivors will be thankful and appreciative for having a job. Rather, often what happens is a sense of resentment mixed with apprehension and insecurity. This may manifest itself as decreased work productivity, increased absenteeism, and other costly indications of unrest. In response to the layoffs that have affected hospitals through the last decade, Steve Cohn (Cerne, 1988), president of Medical Management Planning, Inc., reported "Stress caused by mixed messages, unclear corporate goals, or a shortage of workers can reduce productivity by 20 to 30 percent." Certainly, this statement and these figures apply to any corporate setting be it medical or otherwise.

Managers' Vulnerability

Managers who must decide who is to be laid off are in a vulnerable position. They are often in the position of having much responsibility for following through on the decision, while having little to no authority over the decisions. All psychological research to date indicates that this is a highly stressful position in which to be placed. It is what I refer to as having to make a **"Sophie's Choice,"** if any of you saw the movie by the same name, with Meryl Streep, several years ago. Another metaphor is the **"lifeboat decision"**; who gets in and who must swim? Managers at this level often bear the brunt of any ill will and may go through a variety of reactions to this type of situation.

Most employees currently in management positions initially were trained to provide a service or participate in the manufacturing of a product and did not choose a career of management. Most of them did not receive courses in psychology, personality theory, motivational theory, communication skills, organizational development, etc. The majority came up through the ranks and most received on-the-job training. It is difficult to manage an organization in "good times" and next to impossible in times of crisis. Management is in desperate need of new skills in order to coach their teams through the next years of corporate transition, turmoil, and trauma.

Prescription for Resolution

In my **T.E.A.M. Building** (Techniques to Energize And Motivate) workshops, I discuss the concept of managing with **TLC**: Transitional Leadership, Coaching, Communication, and Commitment. Space does not permit a lengthy discussion, but the following is a summary of some key concepts.

In crisis situations in the workplace, management must include the **Five A's** as key ingredients in any *prescription* for resolution:

ATTITUDE of Open Communication. Management must be willing to provide much information to the "rank and file" regarding any changes, rumors, and questions. They should set up a system through which the employees may address their immediate concerns. Informal meetings, memos, and one-to-one talks are essential.

AWARENESS of Reactions. At times of crisis in the workplace, people respond with a variety of reactions. Managers should have training that will assist them in being able to respond appropriately to employees as they react to the crisis at hand. It is imperative that managers understand that the major part of their job is to manage and lead the people... not just to "get the work out."

AVAILABILITY of Managers and Administrators. During times of crisis and transition, often the tendency is to isolate by groups: managers meet with managers, staff meet with staff. This is often necessary, as much planning usually goes into organizing the upcoming changes. However, the tendency is for camps and cliques to develop within departments. Management must make efforts to maintain a high profile and visibility to the staff. In much the same way that a general goes to the front line to boost the morale of the troops, or a parent is more available to a child who is anxious and insecure, management must be highly visible at times of crisis.

ACKNOWLEDGEMENT of Loss. The organization must recognize that a crisis has occurred and acknowledge the event. One CEO of a large company with whom I was consulting indicated that he would not allow people to *wallow in self-pity*. I explained that acknowledging pain and loss is not self-pity. Further, if someone else provides the acknowledgement, the need would be less for **self**-acknowledgement (self-pity).

APPRECIATION of the Efforts of the Remaining Workers. When people experience a crisis, feelings of loss always occur. To regain a sense of balance and reestablish a feeling of integration and recovery, a sense of trust requires a great deal of effort. Employees must hear positive reactions to their efforts, even if they are "only doing what is expected of them."

I have often heard surprise on the part of management when the *surviving* workers are not appreciative of still having their jobs. Management must be reminded that the surviving workers may have lost friends, have experienced changes in their roles, be working with different people, and in general be feeling threatened. It is not a time to rejoice for what they still have but rather a time to grieve for what has been lost.   A process of mourning must take place before "business as usual" may resume. In the same way that education is not "appreciated" by children, work is not a gift that requires gratefulness. Going to school and to work is something that is expected of us in this society if we are to succeed and live comfortably.

Coping with Transition

Coping with a transition is not a one-sided endeavor in which management is responsible for implementing all of the necessary and appropriate interventions. Many individuals tend to experience **change** as a horrible, evil event that is being forced upon them. They seem to develop a victimized, suspicious view of the events going on and often find themselves in a position of resistance, gathering/giving misinformation, and then feeding the "rumor mill" sometimes knowingly and at other times unknowingly. Employees must allow themselves the time to go through the reactions of **disillusionment** but then return to the task of **reconstruction**. As William Morin, an organizational consultant, indicated, employees must **recognize** that change is taking place, **reconcile** themselves to the new situation, and then **recommit** to the new organization. All efforts must be made to avoid the desire to stay stuck in anger and resentment. This is easier said than done and will take the effort of the entire organization working together (Morin, 1990).

In the face of crisis, trust is often damaged. Patients feel that they cannot trust the MD, children cannot trust their parents, citizens cannot trust the government, and employees cannot trust their management. Disappointment abounds, and trust diminishes. The key issue facing today's organization is how to restore a sense of trust. Trust involves the following:

T—tolerance and time,
R—respect for others and responsibility for self,
U—unity and understanding of purpose/goal/mission,
S—structure/safety, and
T—thoughtfulness.

COMMUNICATION IS THE KEY TO TRUST

Without communication, trust cannot exist; likewise, without trust communication does not occur. *To a large extent, our society does not know how to communicate.* Many of us are quite skilled at talking *at* others; some of us have perfected the fine art of talking *to* another person. Most of us do not know how to talk *with* another person. Most of our society is trained to talk *to* each other. Parents talk to kids, teachers talk to students, clergy talk to congregations, politicians talk to constituents, and managers talk to employees. We become conditioned to one-way communication. **Talking with** another person, be it a professional or personal relationship, is much harder because two-way communication requires listening, understanding, negotiating, and trusting the other.

Humans have an amazing ability to suffer extreme circumstances, take enormous risks, extend themselves for others, and go through terrible crises. They will do it for an idea or cause, to defend their beliefs, to protect themselves and others, or for a person in whom they trust.

Chapter 9

GUIDELINES FOR CONDUCTING DEBRIEFINGS

(and other types of interventions)

As mentioned previously in this manual, debriefing and defusing of critical incidents goes on informally in most police and fire departments, hospitals, and crisis centers. During one of my conferences, a police officer described a shooting incident when he was a young officer. After the incident, the chief of the department took him out for a cup of coffee, and they talked for some time about the event. This type of support goes on in most departments, medical floors, and emergency rooms. It may be a quick discussion accentuated with "gallows humor" or an emotional reaction punctuated by a pat or a hug. More and more ESPs with whom I speak report that they are able to talk with their spouse about the events of the day. This type of **debriefing** is certainly beneficial to both partners in the couple.

Although informal discussions have been a part of the regular day-to-day routine, a **formal debriefing** is a relatively new concept. What qualifies a discussion as a formal debriefing is four components:

1. the meeting is a scheduled event;

2. all members of a designated group are included;

3. usually an outside individual (EAP, peer counselor, mental health professional) who was not involved in the incident, facilitates the debriefing; and

4. the issues of confidentiality and privacy are addressed specifically.

TIMING OF A DEBRIEFING

Regardless of the type of organization or the reason for the debriefing, the general rule is to attempt to conduct a debriefing within three days of the event. However, debriefings may be held up to two to three weeks after an incident. Remember, a late debriefing may be better than no debriefing at all. My belief is that waiting a couple of days to conduct a debriefing may be best for three reasons: (1) an investigation of the event might occur, may add to the crisis, and may need to be processed as part of the debriefing; (2) people may not develop symptoms until a day or two has passed, and a debriefing is more relevant to individuals if they are having some symptoms in order to relate to the discussion; and (3) people may have a need to go home to loved ones or to "get some space" from the event before they feel that they can discuss what has occurred. **The best procedure is to take the time to develop a well planned and structured response (that is delayed a day or two) rather than to have an immediate one that is poorly coordinated and disorganized.**

PRE-INTERVENTION PLANNING

The following are some examples of great efforts that went awry due to insufficient pre-intervention planning.

1. A debriefing session was held in a conference room in which there was a great deal of "traffic" and constant disruption to the process as well as the privacy. In addition to people coming into the room unannounced, phones were ringing that had to be answered.

2. At a debriefing, an argument ensued between two fire service personnel due to a personal conflict because they were each dating the same woman. Their conflict was well known to the department.

3. As a debriefing was getting underway, several of the participants angrily complained that they were forced to be there and had not been told the purpose of the meeting.

4. About two weeks after a well received debriefing, the head of a department called to express his concern about the extra overtime that was spent to pay the participants to attend the debriefing.

5. At a hospital, the psychiatric staff was called to help the ICU with a debriefing around a SIDS case. When the facilitator arrived he found that the hospital chaplain had been called (independently) by one of the staff to "colead" the meeting.

What is becoming increasingly obvious as more debriefings are conducted is the need for pre-intervention planning. The above are a few examples of how a potentially meaningful debriefing may falter, if not fail, as a result of the facilitator(s) not doing his/her (their) "homework." I have heard a variety of accounts where the facilitator walked into a debriefing only to find that the agenda of the participants was quite different than was expected. Or, as is often the case, most organizations have a variety of political tensions and undercurrents. Further, an important procedure is to be sure that the "higher-ups" have given their approval of the process and the arrangements for scheduling, location, and participants.

Figure 9 is a pre-intervention planning form that provides an outline of the essential information necessary prior to initiating a CIS/T response. Gaining this type of data and conducting a pre-intervention planning session may serve to facilitate a more effective and well received intervention.

Also, as discussed in Chapter 7, Reactions of Others, a team should look at the three levels of intervention—*primary*, *secondary*, and *tertiary*, when planning an intervention. As mentioned, intervening at all levels often is not necessary, however, the needs of individuals at all levels should be evaluated.

```
┌─────────────────────────────────────────────────────────────────┐
│ Name of Agency: _____Date:_____   │
│ Type of Agency:_____    │
│ Name of Liaison:_____ Phone:(____)____-_____ │
│ Date and Time of Incident:_____    │
│ Brief Description of Incident:_____    │
│ _____      │
│ _____      │
│ _____      │
│ _____      │
│                                                                  │
│ Other extenuating circumstances:_____     │
│ _____      │
│ Politics/personalities/potential problems:_____     │
│ _____      │
│ _____      │
│                                                                  │
│     Victims:___child___adolescent___adult;                       │
│     ___single___multiple___work-related___nonwork-related;       │
│     ___auto accident___domestic___criminal victimization         │
│     ___act of nature___illness                                   │
│     Others involved: __family__coworkers__bystanders__ESP        │
│                                                                  │
│     What type of response is being requested/suggested?          │
│     ____ individual     ____ small group (less than 8)           │
│     ____ family member(s)  ____ large group (9 to 20 )           │
│     ____ CISD (Critical Incident Stress Disorder) for ESPs       │
│     ____ departmental/organizational                             │
│                                                                  │
│     Other:_____      │
│     Where:_____      │
│     When:_____      │
│     Authority/approval of:_____      │
│ Reminders:                                                       │
│                                                                  │
│     Introduction— Reason for meeting, privacy, no pressure, only involved │
│         participants                                             │
│     "Paint the Picture"— chronological recreation of the event   │
│     Reactions— normalize reactions                               │
│     Education— provide handouts and information through out meeting │
│     Follow-up— ask for participants to report name and phone on follow-up │
│         sheet                                                    │
│                                                                  │
│ Recommendations/follow-up:_____      │
│ _____      │
│ _____      │
│                                                                  │
│ Date:_____   Facilitator:_____       │
└─────────────────────────────────────────────────────────────────┘
```

Figure 9. Pre-intervention planning work sheet.

As mentioned in Chapter 6, Critical Incident Stress Response (CISR): Strategies and Interventions to Deal with CIS, to have the CIS/T response team well organized and coordinated is essential. Planning and training meetings should be conducted on a regular basis. Further, many teams find that to coordinate/communicate with different organizations may be difficult. Often, "turf" concerns may arise as a normal development of the team. Ongoing attention must be directed to managing these issues as they arise. An openness to communicate honestly is essential. Keep in mind, turf issues and inter-team friction is an expected part of team development. It does not mean that the team should be disbanded, but rather that regular attention must be devoted to the maintenance of the team. When I have been asked to consult to a team, I will recommend that the key positions within the team be rotated on a yearly basis. By doing so, all members of the team feel that they have an opportunity to participate at any and all levels.

POST-INTERVENTION DISCUSSION

Of equal importance to the pre-intervention planning is the post-intervention discussion. After each CIS/T response, the team should meet as a group to review the entire intervention. Open discussion about all aspects of the team's performance should be the goal of the post-intervention discussion. In order to achieve this goal, team members need to have a feeling of trust and that they are supported by one another.

COMPONENTS OF A FORMAL DEBRIEFING

The following is an outline of a debriefing model that I have developed over the past several years. Initially it was used for interventions with ESP organizations. However, I have found that it may be adapted easily for utilization with any type of organization and is useful for any size group. Further, it is a model that also may be tailored for intervention with individuals.

Other types of debriefings and interventions will be covered in the latter portion of this chapter.

The formal debriefings that I conduct *are* discussions but with a specific purpose and direction. Although it may appear to be casual and free flowing, my debriefing strategy has five components or phases—introduction, "painting the picture" phase, reaction phase, education phase, and follow-up phase.

Introduction

The debriefing should be started with an explanation as to why the people are gathered together, the purpose of the meeting. If it is a police or fire department, the introductory remarks should be conducted by the chief or a ranking officer. In other types of organizations, a person in a senior administrative capacity should introduce the meeting. If guests, facilitator(s), and/or peer counselors are present, they should be introduced. A statement regarding *confidentiality and privacy* should be made by this senior person. Although the facilitator will repeat the statement about confidentiality, it is essential for the staff of an organization to hear it from *one of their own*. The facilitator(s) should be introduced, *the ball passed to them*, and *the senior staff person should leave... unless they were involved with the incident.*

This process is important because it delivers two very significant messages: (1) being present and introducing the meeting is a statement indicating support and endorsement of the process; and (2) by leaving, the senior person is respecting the privacy of those involved and practicing what was preached—**confidentiality**.

Since the first manual, I have changed my approach to the issue of confidentiality. I no longer request that those in attendance not talk to others about what takes place in the debriefing. I explain that **I** will maintain confidentiality since it is mandated as part of my licensing requirement and my relationship with them. I ask that the participants in the debriefing "respect the rights and privacy of the others." So much of CIS education is telling people that talking to others (spouse, friends, clergy, EAP) is one of the curative methods of coping with

CIS. Often, people will want to talk to others about their experience at the debriefing, and yet they feel conflicted if they have been "sworn to secrecy." Therefore, I ask that if people do talk to others about the debriefing that they (1) limit it to only their "significant others," (2) do not talk to the media, and (3) respect the rights and privacy of the others who have participated in the debriefing.

Prior to the commencement of the debriefing, as people are coming in, getting coffee, etc., I will try to do two things: (1) introduce myself to each one of the people; and (2) give them a copy of a two-page handout entitled either, "Introduction to Critical Incident Stress" or "Introduction to Post-traumatic Stress Disorder" (See **Figure 10** and **Figure 11**). * I feel that it is important to provide these printed materials as they

1. are something that participants can take with them afterwards and share with others,

2. acknowledge the universality of the experience and reactions,

3. begin the education process about CIS and/or PTSD, and

4. allay initial anxiety as to what will take place during meeting.

*In addition, I also include a brief description of the debriefing (See **Figure 12**).

INTRODUCTION TO
CRITICAL INCIDENT STRESS (CIS)
FOR EMERGENCY SERVICE PROFESSIONALS
(ESPs)

IN RECENT YEARS, A LARGE AMOUNT OF RESEARCH HAS BEEN DEVOTED TO CIS IN EMERGENCY SERVICE PROFESSIONALS. THE FOLLOWING IS A BRIEF SUMMARY OF (1) THE TYPES OF SITUATIONS THAT OFTEN CAUSE CIS, (2) THE SIGNS AND SYMPTOMS OF CIS, AND (3) STRATEGIES AND INTERVENTIONS THAT ARE HELPFUL TO INDIVIDUALS COPING WITH CIS.

A CRITICAL INCIDENT IS AN EVENT THAT IS EXTRAORDINARY AND MAY PRODUCE SIGNIFICANT REACTIONS IN ESPs. CIS IS OFTEN THE NATURAL REACTION OF A NORMAL PERSON TO AN EXTREME SITUATION.

CIS MAY MANIFEST ITSELF AS A PHYSICAL, COGNITIVE, AND/OR EMOTIONAL RESPONSE THAT MAY BE EXPERIENCED ALMOST IMMEDIATELY OR MAY BE DELAYED DAYS, WEEKS, OR MONTHS.

MOST ESPs MANAGE THE STRESS OF THEIR CAREER QUITE WELL ON THEIR OWN. HOWEVER, IT HAS BEEN DOCUMENTED THAT PEOPLE WHO UNDERSTAND THE EFFECTS OF CIS AND HAVE A PROCESS BY WHICH TO DISCUSS THE EVENTS AND THEIR REACTIONS OFTEN SPEED UP THE RECOVERY PROCESS, STAY HEALTHIER, REMAIN MORE PRODUCTIVE ON THE JOB, AND HAVE LESS DISRUPTION IN THEIR PERSONAL LIVES.

TYPES OF SITUATIONS THAT MAY RESULT IN CIS
  SINGLE VICTIM INCIDENT(S)

>   Line of duty death of fellow professional
>   Death of a child
>   Serious injury of a child
>   Death of adult (dependent upon circumstances)
>   Threat of violence and/or injury to an ESP
>   Inability of ESPs to intervene and/or perform duties
>   Injury to fellow professional
>   Suicide

Figure 10. Example of a handout distributed to individuals when conducting CIS debriefings.

Figure 10. Continued

MULTI-CASUALTY DISASTER or HIGH INTENSITY LONG DURATION CRISIS

Catastrophic natural event (earthquake, hurricane, etc.)
Transportation accidents
Fires
Hostage situation

SIGNS AND SYMPTOMS OF CIS

PHYSICAL:

- fatigue
- nausea
- muscle tremors
- sweating/chills
- dizziness

COGNITIVE:

- memory impairment
- anomia (word loss)
- difficulty with decision making
- mental confusion
- intrusive thoughts/visions

EMOTIONAL:

anxiety	irritability	grief
fear	remoteness/numbness	hopelessness
guilt	frustration	depression

STRATEGIES AND INTERVENTIONS TO HELP WITH CIS

ONGOING...

Education about CIS as part of training

Availability of CIS debriefings

Open attitude within the department/agency to discuss reactions

Maintenance of good social network

Regular exercise, good diet

Limitation of alcohol and other controlled substances

IF YOU DO EXPERIENCE CIS REACTIONS

Try to eat regularly even if appetite is disturbed.

If sleep is disturbed, do not toss and turn in bed. Read, watch tv, etc.

Do not try to drink away feelings, thoughts, visions...they will diminish in time.

TALK to peer support, an EAP, clergy, spouse, friends, etc.

Remain active and try to maintain regular schedule/activities.

REMEMBER CRITICAL INCIDENT STRESS (CIS) IS THE BODY'S AND MIND'S COPING RESPONSE OF A NORMAL PERSON TO AN ABNORMAL SITUATION. SYMPTOMS WILL RESOLVE; YOU CAN HELP THE PROCESS.

INTRODUCTION TO POST-TRAUMATIC STRESS DISORDER (PTSD)

IN RECENT YEARS A LARGE AMOUNT OF RESEARCH HAS BEEN DEVOTED TO THE EFFECTS OF CRISIS AND TRAUMA ON INDIVIDUALS. THE KNOWN SYNDROME THAT MAY DEVELOP AS A RESULT OF A SIGNIFICANT CRISIS IS CALLED ***POST-TRAUMATIC STRESS DISORDER (PTSD)***. THE FOLLOWING IS A BRIEF SUMMARY OF (1) THE TYPES OF SITUATIONS THAT OFTEN CAUSE REACTIONS, (2) THE SIGNS AND SYMPTOMS OF PTSD, AND (3) STRATEGIES AND INTERVENTIONS THAT ARE HELPFUL TO INDIVIDUALS COPING WITH PTSD.

PTSD MAY RESULT IN RESPONSE TO AN EVENT THAT IS CONSIDERED EXTRAORDINARY AND BEYOND THE SCOPE OF USUAL HUMAN EXPERIENCE. THESE EVENTS MAY PRODUCE SIGNIFICANT REACTIONS IN PEOPLE. PTSD IS OFTEN THE NATURAL REACTION OF A <u>NORMAL</u> PERSON TO AN EXTREME SITUATION.

PTSD MAY MANIFEST ITSELF AS A PHYSICAL, COGNITIVE, AND/OR EMOTIONAL RESPONSE THAT MAY BE EXPERIENCED ALMOST IMMEDIATELY OR MAY BE DELAYED DAYS, WEEKS, OR MONTHS.

IT HAS BEEN DOCUMENTED THAT PEOPLE WHO UNDERSTAND THE EFFECTS OF PTSD AND HAVE A PROCESS BY WHICH TO DISCUSS THE EVENTS AND THEIR REACTIONS OFTEN SPEED UP THE RECOVERY PROCESS, STAY HEALTHIER, REMAIN MORE PRODUCTIVE ON THE JOB, AND HAVE LESS DISRUPTION IN THEIR PERSONAL LIVES.

TYPES OF SITUATIONS THAT MAY RESULT IN PTSD
   SINGLE VICTIM SITUATIONS(S)
      Extreme combat conditions/experience
      Victim/witness of traumatic incident
      Victim/witness of violent crime
      Victim/witness of physical mistreatment
      Victim/witness of sexual mistreatment
   MULTI-CASUALTY DISASTER or HIGH INTENSITY LONG DURATION CRISIS
      Catastrophic natural event (earthquake, hurricane, etc.)
      Transportation accidents
      Fires
      Hostage situation

Figure 11. Example of a handout distributed to individuals in a meeting for PTSD.

Figure 11. Continued

SIGNS AND SYMPTOMS OF PTSD

PHYSICAL:

fatigue

nausea

muscle tremors

sweating/chills

dizziness

COGNITIVE:

memory impairment

anomia (word loss)

difficulty with decision making

mental confusion

intrusive thoughts/visions

EMOTIONAL:

anxiety	irritability	grief
fear	remoteness/numbness	hopelessness
guilt	frustration	depression

STRATEGIES AND INTERVENTIONS TO HELP WITH PTSD:

ONGOING...

Education about PTSD

Availability of PTSD debriefings and on-going counseling

Open attitude within the family/relationships to discuss reactions

Maintenance of good social network

Regular exercise, good diet

Limiting of alcohol and other controlled substances

IF YOU DO EXPERIENCE REACTIONS

Try to eat regularly even if appetite is disturbed.

If sleep is disturbed, do not toss and turn in bed. Read, watch tv, etc.

Do not try to drink away feelings, thoughts, visions...they will diminish in time.

TALK to peer support, an Employee Assistance Program, clergy, spouse, friends,

Remain active and try to maintain regular schedule/activities.

REMEMBER PTSD IS THE BODY'S AND MIND'S COPING RESPONSE OF A NORMAL PERSON TO AN ABNORMAL SITUATION. SYMPTOMS WILL RESOLVE; YOU CAN HELP THE PROCESS.

AN INTRODUCTION TO CRITICAL INCIDENT STRESS/TRAUMA DEBRIEFINGS

In recent years, there has been much focus on the effects of traumatic events on individuals. Oftentimes, people have dramatic reactions to these extraordinary events that may leave them feeling overwhelmed and upset. When a significant crisis occurs, the individuals involved may benefit from an opportunity to talk about the experience as a group. For that reason, "critical incident stress/trauma debriefings" have been promoted as a method to help healing and resolution.

A debriefing is a meeting that, generally, includes only the affected individuals and a facilitator whose responsibility is to provide structure and organization to the meeting. A debriefing is not group therapy but rather is described as a "psycho-educational" experience. A debriefing focuses primarily on the traumatic event and its effects on the individuals, not on personal relationships, personality problems, or professional conflicts. Most importantly, it is not a critique or investigation of what occurred. Nor is it a courtroom to determine guilt or innocence.

The following are some guidelines about today's debriefing:

1. Although you may be encouraged to participate, no one will be forced to talk.
2. I will maintain confidentiality about the meeting. Often, an organization wishes to receive some general feedback about the session. If this is the case, I will discuss this with all of you.
3. Talking about the event that you have been through is an important part of the recovery process. Preferably, you should talk only to family members or "significant others" about the debriefing. If you do so, please protect the privacy of the other participants.
4. Feel free to move around freely to get food and/or beverage or to go to the bathroom. If you do leave the room, please let me know if you will not be returning.
5. The debriefing goes through certain phases. After going over these guidelines, we will start by asking the participants to "paint the picture" by objectively and factually telling the story of what happened. Usually, we try to go in sequence or chronological order as to how the event transpired. Each of you will be asked to describe the event from your perspective. I will ask questions and may, in fact, draw a diagram of the event as we proceed. You may go into as much or as little detail as you wish.
6. After that, I will ask you to describe your reactions at the time of the event and since then. You may want to refer to the other handout to see the "menu" of common reactions to traumatic events.
7. Throughout the debriefing, feel free to ask questions, and I will attempt to answer them as best as possible.
8. Usually these types of meetings last between 1 to 2 hours.
9. There will be follow-up telephone contact with each of you a week or two after this meeting.

Not everyone experiences the same reactions to difficult situations.

The recovery process takes time.

Figure 12. Example of handout distributed to individuals when conducting CIS/T debriefings.

After initial introduction, the facilitator takes charge of the meeting and repeats the introductory orientation in his/her own fashion as the initiation into the debriefing. In addition, often an important procedure is to explain that it is helpful if people will cooperate but that no pressure will be exerted for people to participate in the process. However, even if participants feel that the debriefing is unnecessary for their own welfare, their comments and involvement might be of assistance to someone else in the room. I usually begin the introduction by saying:

The chief (captain, supervisor, etc.) explained why we are meeting today. As many of you know, what you experienced today is considered a very dramatic event that can really affect fire fighters (police, nurses, employees, students, etc.) Talking about this kind of incident is considered "good medicine." Some of you may be thinking that this kind of debriefing is unnecessary. However, even though you may be saying that you don't need this, your comments and participation could be very helpful to someone else in this room. There will be no pressure to participate, but your cooperation certainly would be appreciated by me and most likely by one of your peers (brothers, colleagues, etc.).

Once again I must remind you that what we talk about should be considered private. Talking about the kind of situation that you have experienced is thought to be helpful. If you would find it helpful to discuss the debriefing with your husband, wife, girlfriend, boyfriend, that is ok. However, please remember to use discretion and to respect the rights and privacy of the others. There is to be no discussion with the media, other departments or people who may be loose with their lips.

I have heard that some people conducting debriefings set stringent guidelines about not leaving the room or moving around once the debriefing has begun. I do not make any requests such as these as I want to let people feel as comfortable as possible. Requiring people to stay seated or not leave the room may be experienced as controlling as well as a power move and may antagonize the participants. All efforts are to help individuals regain a sense of control... not to feel controlled. Further, if people are experiencing any discomfort as a result of the debriefing, being able to move around, go to the bathroom, or get a cup of coffee should be tolerated.

As part of the introduction, it is important to clarify that this is not a critique or an investigation. Further, people should limit their comments to their own activities, thoughts, and reactions.

"Painting the Picture" Phase

A discussion is conducted through which the incident is recreated by each individual attempting **objectively and factually** to describe what he/she did as part of the critical incident. This part may be conducted by having people speak randomly; however, I prefer to have the conversation proceed somewhat chronologically. To that end, I initiate the next phase of the debriefing by saying something to this effect:

I hope that everyone understands why we are here, the purpose of the meeting, and the ground rules. I was not at the incident; I know very little about what occurred. I would like you folks to help me to understand what took place, to see what happened at the fire (accident, shooting, drowning, disaster, etc.). I would like to have a vivid picture of the entire incident. When I have done debriefings, the system that works best is what I call "painting the picture." I would like you to describe factually what happened in the order that it happened. So, in a moment, I will ask the first person(s) involved in the incident to describe what happened. This is usually the person who received the call. Then I would like to move to the first person(s) on the scene to describe, if they will, what they did when they arrived at the fire (accident, etc.). People have told me that this is a helpful process because when in a crisis situation, people develop a sense of "tunnel vision"; they become very focused on their own duties and tasks, and, as a result, they often lose a sense of the big picture. So by "painting the picture" for me, you also are helping each other.

During this part of the debriefing, often a remarkable process occurs. People develop a sense of the total gestalt, the whole picture, and find that events transpired of which they were unaware. An example of this was a drowning incident in which three lifeguards were involved. As we painted the picture, the first lifeguard saw the victim struggling and jumped in to assist. The second lifeguard joined him and helped bring the victim into shallow water. The third lifeguard helped them to drag the rather large male person out of the water and initiate CPR. As the third lifeguard described what he did, the second lifeguard had a surprised look on his face. He reported that he was totally unaware that the third lifeguard was there, even though they spoke to each other at the time.

Reaction Phase

After we have gone around and chronologically recreated the critical incident, we then proceed into the next phase in which people are asked to share their **reactions**. I recommend using this word rather than **feelings** because it is more generic and encompasses physiological, cognitive, and emotional responses to the critical incident. Further, focusing on feelings may tend to alienate some participants. Moreover, the discussion of reactions may be generalized more easily to other areas of their lives such as personal relationships. This phase of the debriefing may be introduced by saying:

You folks have done a great job of helping me to get a sense of what took place at the fire (accident, shooting, etc.). I appreciate your openness and willingness to do so.

Often, when people are handling a crisis, they find that they go into "autopilot" mode; they operate automatically without much feeling. This is often an unconscious, protective mechanism that enables people to do a difficult job and do it well. Then, some time after the incident is over, they begin to have reactions. I'd like to go around the room and ask you to comment on what reactions you had while at the incident and what reactions you had after you came off "autopilot." Once again, when it is your turn, please feel free to comment or to pass.

During this phase, I will begin to educate about CIS, presenting a menu of reactions that are considered natural reactions to CIS. This tends to normalize what some may have worried was only their "crazy" reaction. I will introduce this by saying:

Let me describe some of the typical reactions that people often have to a critical incident such as the one that you have described. Some people report having a sense of time distortion. They feel that time is moving either very rapidly or is crawling very slowly.

Others report that they do not experience the victim as a person, but rather as an inanimate object. Some people become aware that they have physical symptoms such as difficulty breathing, shakiness, nausea. Others report having intrusive thoughts and visions where they see a part of the incident every time they close their eyes. On the handout, you will see a list of the common reactions.

Education Phase

Throughout the debriefing, my goal is to educate about CIS. Digressing from the participant's comments, I will use the material to clarify and provide information. It is important to be reassuring and supportive. I provide handouts on CIS or PTSD (see **Figures 10** and **11**). I also allow time for questions and answers.

Follow-up Phase

Before ending the debriefing, I hand out materials including a business card. I tell people that they may feel free to contact me if they would like to talk more about the incident. I also circulate a piece of paper and ask them to record their names and phone numbers so that I might contact them in a few days to see how they are doing and to ask them for feedback about the debriefing. This is important because often people will not initiate a call for assistance but will be responsive to receiving one. It is also another way of indicating that resolving CIS is a process that takes time, not a one-time event that is complete when the debriefing is finished.

Other Components of the Debriefing

Another feature of the debriefings that I conduct is that I try to have some type of food and beverage (nonalcoholic) available during the debriefing. It is never very elaborate—usually coffee, juices, cookies, crackers, etc. A debriefing is a procedure that enables people to deal with loss and grief. Most cultures and religions involve food with the mourning process as eating is a universal practice of nurturance. The process of offering sustenance to another person at a time of crisis is one way of caring for them in a very basic way.

Also, I have found that a nice way to close the debriefing is to offer a brief relaxation exercise. I explain that the debriefing is over, but for those wishing to remain, I will close by leading them through a relaxation procedure. Most professionals facilitating debriefings know of some relaxation procedure that would be appropriate.

OTHER TYPES OF INTERVENTIONS

In the general workplace, a formal debriefing should take place in two types of situations: a serious accident/death in the workplace or a violent crime in the workplace. Other situations that *may* require a formal debriefing are death of coworker outside of work, serious illness of coworker, arrest of or charges pressed against a coworker, suicide attempt/completion of a coworker, "down-sizing," and/or layoff of personnel.

For Injury or Death

In the case of an injury/death in the workplace, the debriefing would be similar to the type that is conducted for ESPs. Often people have witnessed the accident and may have tried to intervene; these people should be attended to immediately, as they would have experienced the most significant impact. As is usually the case, the victim is not present at the debriefings (because they are receiving medical treatment) which allows for the others to participate more freely. Family members of the victim(s) should not be included in this meeting. A separate intervention should be held for family and significant others.

For Victimization by Violent Crime

In the case of victimization by violent crime in the workplace (or as a function of their job), to intervene with the victim individually and to formally debrief others as a group is best. Often people are concerned about their own safety or may want to know how to respond to the victim. At a later time another debriefing may be conducted with the victim and others together. This should *only* be done if the victim feels that it would benefit him/her in some fashion. Regarding suicide, please review Chapter 10, Crises in School Settings.

For Serious Illness or Death of Coworker

In the case of a death or serious illness of a coworker outside of work, I utilize the same "painting the picture" model except this time it is a portrait of the individual. I will introduce the debriefing in the same manner but will amend it as follows:

It would be helpful to me if you could tell me what Mary is/was like. I'd really like you to create as vivid a picture as possible for me—what she looked like physically, her strengths and weaknesses, some anecdotes about her; what you know about her family and any other information that will help me to know her.

I often just go around the room and let people talk freely about the individual. As this phase of the debriefing draws to a close, I will ask people to comment on how the person's illness/death/accident has affected them—what kinds of **reactions** they have had. Often this phase leads to many more feelings and concerns about their own health as well as the feelings of loss of a friend/coworker. This phase may be introduced by:

Thank you for doing such a nice job of describing Mary. I feel that I have a sense of what she looked like as well as her personality. I also know her strengths and weaknesses and a bit about her family. What I'd like to do next is to have you describe your reactions to Mary's illness/death. Many people experience a wide variety of reactions to the serious illness/death of a coworker (if there were extenuating circumstances, then add) *especially given the circumstances surrounding her death. Often people experience a variety of different feelings and reactions; none of them are wrong; they are all natural reactions to a difficult situation.*

My experience has been that this type of debriefing is extremely helpful in situations where people have worked together closely over a period of time. Small departments or groups within a department are vulnerable to experiencing significant reactions to the death/illness of a coworker. We must remember that many people spend more time working, talking, and eating with coworkers than with their own family members. Many share social events or play together on sports teams sponsored by the company. Many develop social lives around the people at work. As I have said before, the workplace is experienced by many as another family. The loss of a coworker may have serious repercussions for others.

For Employees Involved in a Robbery

Several years ago, I was asked to provide an intervention to a bank that had been robbed during the middle of the day. As many of you may know, banks are known for having a significant number of policies and procedures. However, it was discovered that there was no policy should a bank robbery occur. As part of a second debriefing, I asked that the participants give me their suggestions as to what should be included in a policy. The act of becoming "consultants" to the consultant was a very positive one for them. It also helped them to feel acknowledged and empowered. I utilized their suggestions along with input from several other EAPs connected with the banking industry. The following is the policy that I wrote and submitted to the bank administration. It was "passed" and instituted immediately.

It should be noted that a similar policy could be utilized for any type of robbery taking place in a work setting. Convenient stores, retail outlets, etc. often experience robberies that significantly traumatize the employees involved.

1. At the time of a robbery, a bank administrator/officer should go directly to the branch site to (a) be of support to the involved staff, (b) respond to media (if present), and (c) be of assistance to the police investigation.

2. COMPASS (EAP, etc.) should be notified immediately and group and/or individual debriefings should be arranged ASAP to take place after police investigation.

3. A bank administrator/officer should assist branch staff in contacting family/significant others. It is important for involved staff not to be left alone or to go home to an empty residence.

4. Involved staff should be accompanied to police station and/or hospital (if required).

5. Involved staff should be offered time off (maximum of one-to-two days) before returning to work. Preferably, a debriefing will take place during this time.

6. A statement should go to other bank employees/branches describing the incident and what policy/procedures took place. By doing so, it will limit effects of the "rumor mill."

7. An optional debriefing should be made available to non-involved employees as a robbery at one branch may precipitate apprehension throughout the system.

8. A senior bank administrator/officer should meet with involved staff one to two weeks after the incident to discuss their reactions.

9. Follow-up interventions by COMPASS (EAP) to be arranged as required.

10. An optional debriefing should be offered to families of the involved staff members.

For Employees Involved in a Corporate Restructuring

The aforementioned model also may be utilized in the case of helping employees deal with a layoff, downsizing, or some other type of transition in the workplace. For further information about this type of situation, please refer to Chapter 8, Trauma and Crises in the Workplace.

NOTE TO EMPLOYEE ASSISTANCE PROFESSIONALS

• Gain training in the area of CIS/T Response!

• Do not feel that you must call in an *expert* to handle a crisis. (However, if you feel that your training is limited, you may want to contract an outside person to conduct the debriefing. This individual should be seen as an adjunct to yourself; you should be viewed as responsible for the CIS/T response.)

- *Remember, resolution of a crisis/trauma/disaster is not an event, but rather an ongoing process.*

- You need to remain active and involved long after the outside *expert* has left.

- It is advantageous for you as an EAP to be trained in CIS/T Response because bringing in a consultant may result in a loss in credibility of the position of an EAP.

- Take responsibility for formulating policy and procedures.

- Develop drafts that these policies and procedures that may be circulated to the administration of the organization.

- Promote training programs for your client/company that cover CIS/T.

- Use resources available to you

- Call other EAPs that may have more/other experience in dealing with CIS/T.

THE DIFFERENCE BETWEEN A CIS/T RESPONSE AND OTHER MENTAL HEALTH INTERVENTIONS

CIS/T interventions utilize many of the same counseling skills and techniques that most health professionals develop during their training and career. However, there are significant differences between CIS/T interventions and the "usual and customary" clinical services provided by mental health, EAP, and other professionals. Often, formal clinical training does not prepare one for the types of situations that require a CIS/T response because they are so different from the "typical" clinical case. A CIS/T response is not psychotherapy. Psychotherapy usually is sought by an individual as a **reactive** response to emotional symptoms. The intent of a CIS/T response is **proactive**, usually initiated administratively for a group of individuals. The involved individuals are not "patients" or "clients," but rather participants. The focus only is to look at the incident in which participants were involved and their reactions to it. The time is not for reviewing the psychosocial histories nor for delving into personal relationship issues. A CIS/T response is a **situation specific** and **time limited** intervention with a group of participants defined by their involvement in a unique event. Many clinicians are trained to work with individuals and couples, in long-term psychotherapy, with a nondirective style, in the structure of a 50-minute session, in the comfort of his/her own office. Often, the CIS/T intervention takes place outside of the confines of one's office which may add increased anxiety. In addition, a CIS/T intervention requires that the facilitator be active and directive in his/her style. Figure 13 summarizes the differences between a CIS/T response and other clinical interventions.

CIS/T Response	Psychotherapy
proactive response	reactive response
not psychotherapy	uses various theoretical treatment modalities
includes "work" group	includes "significant others" (family, couples, etc.)
situation specific	attempts to relate current situation to past history
time limited intervention	no specific time/session limit
active/directive approach	approach varies with problem/professional training
no focus on psychosocial history	uses psychosocial history
emphasizes coping strategies	goal is to alter chronic behavior patterns
usually conducted outside of clinical setting	conducted in clinical setting
food and beverage served	usually no food and beverage served
no direct payment from participants	client and/or responsible person pay for the services

Figure 13. Summary of the differences between a CIS/T response and other clinical interventions

Chapter 10

CRISES IN SCHOOL SETTINGS

I have devoted a separate chapter to dealing with crises in school settings principally (no pun intended) due to the fact that the primary residents of a school are children. For many children, a school may become a surrogate family with a variety of adults to whom a child may grow very attached. The obvious adults are the teachers and principal(s). However, anyone who has young children knows the potential importance of the office secretary, guidance counselor, school nurse, crosswalk safety person, cafeteria worker, custodian, and bus driver.

Over the years, I have consulted to several school systems and have observed personally at least one, if not several, instances of each of the following events: suicide attempt by student, suicide completion by student, suicide completion by student on school grounds, serious injury of student in a car accident, death of student in a car accident, serious illness of teacher(s), death of teacher outside of school, death of teacher on school property, death of parent while student is in school, murder of student's mother, teacher charged with inappropriate sexual behavior by student, teacher being asked to resign as a result of inappropriate behavior, teacher assaulted by student, and a student assaulted by another student. All of these incidents certainly had far-reaching impact on the infrastructure of the school. When one takes into account the parents, municipality, and media, an event in or involving a school system affects the totality of the community.

Time does not permit ample discussion of all the aforementioned incidents. My experience has been that a suicide of a student is a most serious incident with an extensive impact on the entire community. Therefore, I have chosen to discuss appropriate responses to a suicide or a serious suicide attempt. Most of the guidelines for handling a suicide also would apply to the other types of crises in school settings. Further, some of the following guidelines would be appropriate to consider if a suicide attempt/completion occurs in a work setting. It is recommended that other policies and procedures be developed for other types of crises that are tending to occur in school settings at an increasingly greater frequency.

SUICIDE AMONG ADOLESCENTS

In recent years, much attention has been paid to the well-documented fact that suicide among adolescents is increasing at an alarming rate. Several studies provide the following sample of statistics: from 1961 to 1975, the overall suicide rate increased 22% while the suicide rate of the 15- to 24-year-old age group increased by 131%. Reported in another study done in the mid-1950s to 1978, the suicide rate for this age group more than tripled. In less than two decades, suicide has moved from the fifth leading cause of death among 15- to 24-year-olds and is now ranked second only to accidents. Certainly some of this increase may be the result of more accurate reporting by police, hospitals, and family. However, the disclosure factor does not account fully for the dramatic increase; most researchers believe that underreporting still has a deflating impact on the suicide statistics.

CATEGORIES OF SELF-HARMING BEHAVIOR

During my 10 years as Chief Psychologist on a psychiatric unit, in my private practice, and through my consultations, what has become apparent is that teenagers hurt themselves through a variety of different methods for a myriad of reasons. For me, a helpful procedure has been to differentiate four categories of self-harming behavior: ***self-harming gesture, physical mutilation, self-destructive activity, suicide attempt.*** Many people have a tendency to lump these behaviors all under suicide. It is my feeling that each of these types of self-harming behavior has a different motivation (conscious or otherwise) and therefore requires a different response and level of intervention. The purpose of this manual is *not* to focus on the etiology of suicidal intent nor to discuss clinical interventions, but rather to describe how a school system should respond to this type of incident. However, some understanding of the four different types of self-harm is needed so that a school system may respond differently to each.

Self-harming Gesture

This describes an activity in which some degree of trauma is initiated by the individual. However, the level of objective lethality (actual potential harm of the activity) is low, the individual does the activity in a setting where the likelihood of intervention is strong (i.e., school, home, friend's house), or he/she immediately seeks out attention. Examples of self-harming gestures would be cutting one's arm with a safety razor, taking an overdose in the school bathroom, and hurting one's self while talking to a friend on the phone.

Individuals involved in this type of activity may choose school as the place to do the gesture. Often, school personnel become very concerned that this is a sign that the school is doing something incorrectly (if a child overdoses in the bathroom, etc.). It is my belief that this, in fact, represents just the opposite. It is practically impossible to kill one's self in a school setting; a child choosing to hurt him/herself in school is obviously seeking attention and knows that the school system will respond.

Physical Mutilation

This describes an activity in which the individual chooses to hurt himself/herself but does not have any intention of ending his/her own life. Often it involves painful, but low lethality, trauma such as burning with cigarettes or lighters, multiple cutting over different parts of the body (but with limited severity), or smashing hand/fist into walls or doors. The individual chooses to physically hurt himself/herself in an effort to relieve psychological pain. To describe this in more detail would require a great deal more clinical elaboration, which is not the purpose of this manual. A physical mutilation is not a suicidal act, but often is an attempt to feel alive, to be rid of psychological numbness.

Self-destructive Behavior

This describes activities that are certainly harmful and may, in fact, result in serious injury or death. However, the primary motivation is not to inflict bodily harm to one's self. Examples of self-destructive behavior may include driving to endangerment while under the influence of alcohol, mixing a variety of drugs and alcohol, being in dangerous places or with dangerous people, anorexia, sexual promiscuity, etc.

Suicide Attempt

This describes a serious effort to end one's life. The objective lethality of the activity is high (gun, hanging, jumping), leaving limited time for a change of mind or intervention by others. The individual chooses a place or time of isolation (woods, home alone, after family has gone to sleep). Intervention is usually by accident, and there is a general feeling that the individual was quite serious about wanting to end his/her life.

SCHOOL PROTOCOL

Certainly much more could be said about the self-harming activities of children. Despite increased awareness, training, experience, expertise, and research, young people still choose to end their lives in greater numbers than ever before. The school system does not have the responsibility to assess the level of suicidality or into what category of self-harm an activity may be assigned. Also, the school system does not have the responsibility to diagnose or treat the vulnerable children. School personnel must realize that they are in a profession that puts them in contact with children at risk and that there will be casualties during the course of their careers. I have worked with several school systems in developing an "administrative protocol" to be utilized in the case of self-harming behavior. This protocol represents a clearly defined, structured chain-of-command procedure that facilitates communication and rapid response. Additionally, and of equal importance, this protocol defines each professional's responsibility. It is a step-by-step walk-through describing the following:

1. a brief description of clinical signs and symptoms of children at risk;

2. a statement regarding student-teacher confidentiality, when it must be broken and how to explain this to the child (I have seen teachers caught in the bind of "I'll kill myself if you tell anyone..." or "I'll deny that I told you...");

3. agency hierarchy—designation of responsibility for making certain decisions;

4. how to facilitate clinical backup/evaluation/hospitalization; and

5. who will communicate with parents, students, and media and how will that communication be handled.

In 1985, as part of my consultation with a local school system, I worked in collaboration with the school social worker to develop a protocol for that school system. The following is an edited version of that protocol. It should be noted that this school system decided to utilize the guidance staff rather than school social workers, nurses, or other pupil personnel staff. This is not a comment on skill or preference, but rather is due to the fact that there are guidance departments in each school and that each student is assigned to a guidance counselor.

The following is a plan for helping seriously depressed and/or suicidal students:

1. If a school employee becomes aware of a student at risk, that employee should notify the student's guidance counselor. If the student talks directly to the school employee about his/her feelings, that employee should not

make bargains about not telling the guidance counselor; to do so makes that employee a hostage to emotional blackmail. Further, school personnel are considered mandated to report indications of harm befalling students whether it be self-inflicted or otherwise. This should be explained to the student very carefully. If the student has made actual verbal statements about being suicidal in the employee's presence, the student should be taken directly to the guidance office. The employee should stay with the student until the guidance counselor is available. If the student has done any harm to himself/herself, the school nurse also should be involved.

2. The guidance counselor should attempt to do an evaluation of the situation. Efforts should be made to determine how serious the student is about hurting himself/herself. (Most guidance departments have received training/consultation in this area.) The guidance counselor should explain to the student that the counselor takes this very seriously and that it is school policy that the principal be notified. The student also should be made aware that the principal probably will notify a parent. The student should be allowed to indicate which parent he/she would prefer to be notified.

3. The principal should be told of the situation and should call the parent, gently explain the circumstances, and insist that at least one parent comes to the school.

4. While awaiting contact with and arrival of the parent(s), the guidance counselor should stay with the student at all times. Efforts should be made to plan with the student how the meeting with the parents will go and any plans for further evaluation.

5. When the parent(s) arrive(s) the guidance counselor and principal should *help the student* tell his/her parent(s) about his/her feelings. Efforts also should be made to support the parents, as they may be shaken by the incident.

6. The principal/guidance counselor then should assist the parent(s) in making arrangements to have the student taken to a clinic/hospital/therapist for further evaluation. Even if the parent(s) and child are denying the seriousness of the

incident, it should be explained that the school deems this necessary from a liability standpoint.

7. A release of information should be signed by the parent enabling the school personnel to talk with the evaluating agency.

8. In some cases, the parent(s) may refuse to follow through with further evaluation. It should be explained to the parent(s) that their refusal to get the evaluation may be interpreted as not providing adequate care and protection for their child. It has been well-documented that many children who hurt themselves are often the victims of physical and/or sexual abuse. The parents may be trying to avoid further evaluation because they are fearful of disclosure. At this point, the principal must make a decision as to whether a social service agency should be contacted. All efforts should be made to avoid such a confrontation, as this will have far-reaching impact. Further, the school superintendent should be made aware of the situation if it reaches this juncture.

9. Parents should be told that the school would like a written statement from the evaluation indicating that the child is safe to return to school.

10. A follow-up phone call should be made to the home later in the day/evening to see how things went and when the child might be returning to school.

11. All personnel involved with the incident should meet to debrief about the management of the individual, how it will be handled in the school, and their own feelings and reactions.

12. The incident should be documented by the guidance counselor, describing all the steps that were taken and recommendations that were made.

13. Prior to returning to school, a meeting should be held among school personnel, parent(s), and the child to discuss the transition back into school. Often, the child is quite anxious regarding what has been told to classmates, how they will receive him/her, etc. Plans should be made for

increased support from guidance and other pupil personnel staff.

Certainly, these are very basic components to a school protocol that must go through the proper endorsement by the administration and school committee.

PROTOCOL FOR DEATH OR SUICIDE

Over the years, I have received many questions regarding what is the *right way* to handle a death/suicide of a student. Here are some guidelines that I usually recommend that may be modified to suit the specific system and situation.

1. Design a *telephone chain* so that all school staff may be notified quickly in the case of a crisis.

2. Schedule an information and planning session for school personnel as soon as possible. The school staff needs to (a) be given accurate information, (b) be able to give consistent information to all students, and (c) be able to assist in the response planning. This session may act as a debriefing for the school staff as a way of helping them deal with their reactions.

3. Avoid large assemblies as a way to disseminate information to the student body. Assemblies are too impersonal and do not allow for discussion or expression of reactions on the part of students. Further, to another student in the audience who may be feeling similar depressive feelings, an assembly may appear to be *attention* given to the student who hurt himself/herself and thus, might make self-harming behavior more appealing to those students who remain at risk.

4. Talk to classmates, close friends and peers of the individual in a casual and informal manner. This method is most suitable. Enlist their efforts to reach out to others who they think may be "hurting" as a result of the incident. Do not make them feel that they must be the counselor, but rather the messenger that lets people know that help is available.

5. Have "drop-in" discussions available throughout the week at different times during the school schedule.

6. Designate one school administrator as the **information coordinator** for media and parent concerns.

7. **Do not** immediately add the topic of suicide/death to the school curriculum. If there is a desire to address this as part of the academic content it should be done in the context of looking at values clarification, psychology, or dealing with difficult feelings. Too often, I have seen faculty respond to a crisis by wanting to make it an academic course. Addressing suicide without embedding it within a larger context is similar to having a course on pregnancy without discussing sexual reproduction, emotional relationships, child rearing, birth control, etc.

8. Unless it is a small school in which everyone knew the student, **do not** cancel school. However, all efforts should be made to allow those students who wish to attend the funeral, or need to take time for themselves, to do so without concern about schoolwork.

9. Provide a means for expression of feelings. Letters of condolence to the family of the deceased student may be prepared as in-class work; or perhaps a group of students may be organized and supported to make some type of mural in the school in memory of the student.

10. Send a formal notice to parents in order that they be informed regarding the incident and the school's response; also, the notice should further advise parents to be aware of their children's reactions.

Schools are unique settings, requiring special treatment if a crisis occurs. Without question, appropriate interventions must be conducted. The best procedure is to have guidelines in place prior to any crisis. As we all know, the middle of a crisis is not the best time to be creating protocol.

Figure 14 provides guidelines for crisis management, and **Figure 15** provides a crisis intervention data form that I designed for a school system to which I have been consulting for several years. The school is an "alternative" high school enrolling a wide variety of students with an equally wide variety of emotional difficulties. Although more crises tend to be in this type of school, policies and forms such as these should be part of any school system's policies and procedures manual.

GUIDELINES FOR CRISIS MANAGEMENT

Recent budgetary constraints and philosophical shifts have resulted in an increase in the number of referrals to alternative educational programs. Further, many programs are finding a different type of student on the roster and in the classroom than in previous years. Greater numbers of students are (1) from seriously dysfunctional families, (2) transitioning from residential treatment programs, and (3) involved with the legal system.

During the course of any school year, the attention of the staff may be called to a student who may be experiencing some type of crisis in his/her life. Or, a crisis may develop during any school day. This could be an accident, an illness, drug involvement, serious medical or psychiatric symptoms, or a serious disciplinary incident.

The following are guidelines regarding crisis management in the _____ school department. The _____ school is an alternative academic setting that provides school adjustment counseling. It is not a psychiatric facility nor a residential treatment program that provides clinical treatment.

GUIDELINES

It is imperative that the "sending schools" and families provide the _____ school with as much information about the students as possible. This is especially the case if a student is coming out of a residential and/or hospital setting. Often students come to the school with little to no accompanying information.

An informational data form will be completed on each student by the staff and/or psychological consultant. It will summarize psychosocial information, psychological treatment status, medical information, etc.

If any staff member gains knowledge of or has reason to believe that a student is threatening to hurt or is assessed to be at risk of hurting himself/herself, the staff immediately will notify the principal. He/she will assess the situation by meeting with the student. If he/she feels that the student is at risk, the following consultation options are available: (1) the director; (2) the "sending school" Special Education Department liaison; (3) a psychological consultant; and (4) the student's parent or guardian.

Even "trivial" incidents may be considered "warning signs" and should be evaluated by the staff.

If a staff member becomes aware that a student (1) has become seriously ill, (2) has had an accident, (3) intentionally has hurt himself/herself; (4) has ingested drugs/alcohol and is "under the influence," or (5) has or is experiencing serious psychiatric and/or medical symptoms, the principal **must** choose one of the aforementioned options available for consultation.

As the school setting is not equipped to deal with serious crises, efforts will be made to arrange for the student(s) to be removed from the school. Disposition planning may include (1) sending the student home with parent/guardian, (2) calling police/ambulance, or (3) taking the student to the hospital for immediate evaluation.

Please understand, our primary goal is to provide a safe environment in which the student can acquire academic training.

Figure 14. Example of guidelines for crisis management in a school.

CRISIS INTERVENTION DATA FORM

STUDENT'S NAME:_____ DATE:_____

If more than one:_____

_____

TYPE OF INCIDENT:_____ DATE:_____TIME:_____

_____ injury/illness _____ disciplinary/misbehavior

_____ potential risk of harm to self/others _____ Other_____

BRIEFLY DESCRIBE THE INCIDENT: _____

_____

_____

_____

_____

INTERVENTIONS: (Please check all that apply to the situation.)

_____ spoke with student

_____ consulted with principal

_____ directed student to principal

_____ consulted with psychological consultant

_____ consulted with SPED liaison from student's school: _____

_____ spoke with student's parent/guardian: _____

_____ requested emergency services:_____

_____

_____ dismissed student with parent/guardian

_____ dismissed student (over 18 years of age)

_____ other. Please describe: _____

_____

_____

_____

PLAN OF ACTION: (Please document the results of and recommendations from the interventions above. Also indicate a plan of action.)

_____

_____

_____

_____

_____

_____

Staff signature

Figure 15. Example of a crisis intervention data form.

SUMMARY

In closing, a most important point to remember is that recovery from crisis, disaster, and trauma is not an event, but rather a process. For the individual victim, it takes much time to reestablish a renewed sense of self, balance, and wholeness. For Emergency Service Professionals, an ongoing awareness needs to be maintained that ESPs have chosen a line of work that may place them in situations that are beyond the typical. Further, departments must devote time and training to areas of stress and Critical Incident Stress Response.

Unfortunately, crises, trauma and disasters always will occur. As a result, plenty of work needs to be done. Good luck, assist others, and take care of yourselves.

BIBLIOGRAPHY

BIBLIOGRAPHY

American Psychiatric Association. (1987). *Diagnostic and statistical manual of mental disorders* (third edition, revised). Washington, DC: Author.

Barnett, A. (1960). *People under pressure.* Schenectady, NY: New College & University Press.

Blanchard, K., & Johnson, S. (1982). *The one minute manager.* New York, NY: Morrow Publishing.

Cerne, F. (October 5, 1988). Hospitals not immune to high cost of stress. *Hospital* 62 (9), 69-70.

Covey, S. (1990). *The seven habits of highly effective people.* New York, NY: Simon & Schuster.

Crane, S. (1987). *The red badge of courage.* In Puffin Classic Series. New York, NY: Penguin Books. (Original work published 1885)

Centers for Disease Control. (1984). Leading work-related diseases and injuries—United States. *U.S. Morbidity and Mortality Weekly Report, 33,* 3-5.

Centers for Disease Control. (1987). Traumatic occupational fatalities—United States, 1980-1984. *U.S. Morbidity and Mortality Weekly Report, 36,* 725-727.

Demi, A., & Miles, M. (1983). Understanding physiologic reactions to disaster. *Journal of Emergency Nursing, 9,* 11-16.

Doran, M. (1988). Managing ICU-induced stress. *American Journal of Nursing, 88,* 1559-62.

Everly, G. (1989). *A clinical guide to the treatment of the human stress response.* New York, NY: Plenum Press.

Everly, G., & Feldman, R. (1985). *Occupational health promotion: Health behavior in the workplace.* New York, NY: Chevron Publishing.

Executive Development III. (1982). *Areas of emergency stress that affect fire fighters.* An unpublished nationwide study of the National Fire Academy. Washington, DC.

Executive Development III. (1984). *A model EAP for all emergency response and associated personnel.* An unpublished research project for the National Fire Academy. Washington, DC.

Faberow, N., & Frederick, C. (1978). *Training manual for human service workers in major disasters.* Washington, DC: U.S. Government Printing Office.

Fletcher, J. (1987). Stress management. *Intensive Care Nursing, 3,* 56-60.

Frederick, C. (1987). Crisis intervention and emergency mental health. In W. Johnson (Ed.), *Health Action.* Fort Worth, TX: Holt, Rinehart, & Winston.

Frankl, Viktor. (1966). *Man's search for meaning.* NY: Washington Square Press.

Freud, S. (1989). *Civilization and its discontents.* J. Strachey (Ed.). New York, NY: Norton Press.

Freud, S. (1957). Mourning and melancholia. In *A general selection from the works of Sigmund Freud,* edited by John Riekman. NY: Doubleday.

Freudenberger, H. (1980). *Burn-out: The high cost of achievement.* New York, NY: Anchor Press.

Herman, J. (1992). *Trauma and recovery.* NY: Basic Books.

Hermann, S. (1989, November). Psychosomatic injuries: How common are they? *Fire Command,* pp. 12-14.

Hodgman, C. (1985). Recent findings in adolescent depression and suicide. *Journal of Developmental and Behavioral Pediatrics (JDBP)*, *6*, 3.

Holinger, P. (1978). Adolescent suicide: An epidemiological study of recent trends. *American Journal of Psychiatry*, *135*, 6.

Innes, J, & Clarke, A. (1985, September 2). The response of professional fire-fighters to disaster. *Disasters*, pp. 149-153.

Ivancevich, J., & Matteson, M. (1987). *Controlling work stress.* New York, NY: Josey-Bass.

Johnson, J. (1987, November 2). Critical incident stress: Healing the victim and the caregivers. *Emergency Nursing Report*, pp. 1-8.

Kubler-Ross, E. (1970). *On death and dying.* New York, NY: Macmillan Books.

Lawrence, R., & Lawrence, S. (1987-88). The nurse and job related stress: Response, RX and self-dependency. *Nursing Forum*, 23, (2), 45-51.

Lenehan, G.P. (1986, December). Emotional impact of trauma. *Emergency Nursing Clinics of North America*, p. 21.

Mitchell, J., & Resnik, H.L.P. (1981). *Emergency response to crisis.* Ellicott City, MD: J. Mitchell.

Morin, William. (1990). *Trust me.* NY: Harcourt Brace Jovanovich.

Muller, P. (1987, February). Avoiding burnout through prevention. *Journal of Post Anesthesia Nursing*, *2*(1), 53-58.

Murphy, L., & Schoenborn, T. (1987, May). *Stress management in work settings.* Washington, DC: U.S. Department of Health and Human Services.

Osterkamp, L, & Press, A. (1988). *Stress? Find your balance.* Lawrence, KS: Preventive Measures.

Pelletier, K. (1977). *Mind as healer, mind as slayer.* New York, NY: Delta Books.

Peters, T. & Waterman, R. (1988). *In search of excellence: Lessons from America's best run companies.* New York, NY: Warner Books.

Pierson, T. (1988, Summer). Critical incident stress and the tactical team. *The Tactical Edge,* pp. 26-27.

Robbins, A. (1986). *Unlimited power.* New York, NY: Ballantine Books.

Selye, H. (1978). *The stress of life.* New York, NY: McGraw Hill.

Shafii, M., Carrigan, S., Whittinghill, J., & Derrick, A. (1985). Psychological autopsy of completed suicide in children and adolescents. *American Journal of Psychiatry, 142*(9), 1061-4.

van der Kolk, B. (1987). *Psychological trauma.* Washington, DC: American Psychiatric Press.

Violent deaths among persons 15 to 24 years of age. (1983). *U.S. Morbidity and Mortality Weekly Report, 34,* 453-7.

Zigler, Zig. (1987). *Top performance: How to develop excellence in yourself & others.* New York, NY: Berkley Publishing.

INDEX

INDEX

ABOUT
THE
AUTHOR

Gerald W. Lewis

Gerald Lewis is a clinical psychologist practicing in the Boston area for the past 15 years. He received his doctorate from the George Washington University in 1977.

He was the Chief Psychologist at the Marlboro Hospital for nine years and remains on the medical staff.

In 1985, he went into private practice and as codirector organized **MetroWest Mental Health Associates (currently named, Mental Health Affiliates of Marlboro and Framingham)**, a multidisciplinary group of mental health professionals.

In 1986, in an effort to combine his clinical experience with his training and consultation skills, he founded **COMPASS--Comprehensive Assessment and Consultation**, as a means of providing Employee Assistance Programs, consultation, and training services.

Dr. Lewis has given more than 100 presentations to treatment agencies, schools, and other organizations on a wide variety of mental health, work, and family issues.

Recently, he has been focusing his attention on **Critical Incident Stress and Trauma in the Workplace,** addressing professional audiences through out the country. He is a guest lecturer of the Massachusetts Fire Fighters Academy. He is also Assistant Team Coordinator of the MASSPORT CISD Team. He is a member of the Disaster Response Network and serves as the Coordinator of Training for the Massachusetts chapter.

Gerry lives in Framingham, Massachusetts with his wife, Jo, and their two sons, Aaron and Jacob.

ABBREVIATIONS

ASAP — As Soon As Possible
CEO — Chief Executive Officer
CI — Critical Incident
CIS — Critical Incident Stress
CISD — Critical Incident Stress Disorder
CISR — Critical Incident Stress Response
CIS/T — Critical Incident Stress/Trauma
COMPASS — Comprehensive Assessment and Consultation
CNS — Central Nervous System
CPR — Cardiopulmonary Resuscitation
DSM — Diagnostic and Statistical Manual of Mental Disorders
EAP — Employee Assistance Professional
— Employee Assistance Program
EMT — Emergency Medical Technician
ER — Emergency Room
ESP — Emergency Service Professional
Five A's — Attitude, Awareness, Availability, Acknowledgement, Appreciation
haz mat — Hazardous Materials
HEW — U.S. Department of Health Education and Welfare
HIV — Human Immunodeficiency Virus
ICU — Intensive Care Unit
MD — Medical Doctor
PMA — Positive Mental Attitude
PPP — Policies, Procedures, Programs
PTSD — Post-traumatic Stress Disorder
RN — Registered Nurse
RPM — Respirations per minute
SIDS — Sudden Infant Death Syndrome
SPED — Special Education
T.E.A.M. —Techniques to Energize and Motivate
TLC — Transitional Leadership Coaching, Communication, and Commitment
WWII — World War II